MOON
OF OTHER
DAYS

'THE BALLAD OF EAST AND WEST'

M·M·KAYE'S
KIPLING

A SELECTION OF
FAVOURITE VERSES WITH
NOTES AND SKETCHES
BY M·M·KAYE

AND PAINTINGS BY
GEORGE SHARP

HODDER AND STOUGHTON
LONDON · SYDNEY · AUCKLAND · TORONTO

Printed in Hong Kong for Hodder and Stoughton Limited.
Mill Road, Dunton Green, Sevenoaks, Kent
Hodder and Stoughton Editorial Office:
47 Bedford Square, London WC1B 3DP

British Library Cataloguing in Publication Data
Kipling, Rudyard.
Moon of other days: M.M. Kaye's Kipling:
favourite verses
I. Title   II. Kaye, M.M.
821′.8   PR4851
ISBN 0-340-40302-0

CONTENTS

To

GOFF
(Ob. Dec. 1985)

———

Never again in Rida'ar, my watch-fire burning,
That he might see from afar, shall I wait his returning;
...
Never again in Rida'ar! My ways are made black to me!
Whether I sing or am silent, he shall not come back to me!
There is no measure for trial, nor treasure for bringing.
Allah divides the Companions. (*Yet he said – yet he said:–*
    'Cease not from singing.')

        Kipling: *A Song in the Desert*

Illustration from an original oil painting
by Major General Goff Hamilton CB, CBE, DSO

FOREWORD

By M·M·Kaye

ONCE UPON a half-term holiday — which as a schoolgirl I was spending in my grandfather's house because my parents were in India — I came across several bound volumes of a long-defunct Victorian magazine, and leafing through them was fascinated to discover an article in praise of a new young writer called Rudyard Kipling.

New–? It was difficult to visualize Kipling as a new writer, for having been brought up on the *Just So Stories* and *The Jungle Books,* to me he had been around for ever. But the article described him as a bright nova in the literary sky and said that only time would show whether he would prove to be a planet or a meteor — or words to that effect. I can only recall the gist of it. And I presume I wouldn't even remember that if I hadn't looked up *nova, planet* and *meteor* in a dictionary to sort out which was what! But having done so, the information, and the incident, stuck; and it was gratifying to know that the writer of that article (no astronomer, as you can see!) would not have had long to wait before discovering that the 'nova' *was* a spectacular planet and no shooting star.

Personally, I wouldn't describe Kipling as a star, because nowadays stars, though they twinkle prettily on clear nights, make me think of pop-idols and press agents, and there was precious little prettiness about *Soldiers Three* or *Danny Deever*! Nor did the young Kipling exactly twinkle: on the contrary, his initial impact on London's literary scene appears to have been more like that of a Catherine wheel going off in the middle of a sedate Victorian tea-party, so a sun might have been a more appropriate simile. Except that there is not much mystery, magic, or romance about sunlight, while Kipling's stories are full of all three: as witness the enchanted tales in *Puck of Pook's Hill* and *Rewards and Fairies.* Moonlight, on the other hand, can make anything look beautiful — and fill every shadow with mystery or menace. And that is why I decided to use the title of one of his own verses, and call this very personal selection of Kipling's verse *Moon of Other Days.* For after all, his day is long over and done with; and he illuminated it with a lovely light.

'Ah, Moon of my delight that knows no wane', wrote Omar Khayyam. And as far as I am concerned the delight that much of Kipling's work gave me has never waned, for I still read and re-read it over and over again. Not all of it, because I have to admit that some of it I dislike intensely, and that some of the things he said, did and wrote were enough to draw an agonised *Ouch!* from even the most fervent of his admirers — of which I am one. But then a good many geniuses have had a dislikeable streak in them: Mozart for one! And so what? Personally, I can forgive Kipling anything for the sake of *Kim* alone. Or when it comes to poetry, for *Cities and Thrones and Powers.* And, more recently, for something he wrote to his last surviving aunt when the old lady was dying and he himself — though he cannot have known it then — had only sixteen more days to live: 'He who put us into this life does not abandon His own work for any reason or default at the end of it. That is all I have come to learn out of my life.' Thank you for those words, dear Ruddy. I needed them.

Some years ago I wrote a historical novel, set in 19th century India, in which I included a number of real-life characters and a good many real-life incidents: among the latter the disastrous attempt by a squadron of the 10th Hussars to cross a ford on the Kabul River by night and when the river was rising. Forty-six of them out of a total of seventy-five were drowned that night. And only three years later a bespectacled teenager, not yet seventeen, one Rudyard Kipling — who would one day write their lament in verses that you will find in this book — landed in Bombay, en route to the ancient Mogul city of Lahore, where his father Lockwood Kipling, curator of the Lahore Museum, had found him a job as assistant editor on the staff of an English-language newspaper, the *Civil and Military Gazette*.

Rudyard's father was not only an artist, but a sculptor, an architect, a craftsman and a scholar. His mother was one of the beautiful Macdonald sisters; two of whom married well-known artists who were subsequently knighted — Sir Edward Burne-Jones and Sir Edward Poynter. A third sister married a rich iron master and became the mother of a future Prime Minister; the Stanley Baldwin who was to have the unenviable task of dealing with the abdication of Edward VIII, better known as the Duke of Windsor.

Rudyard's mother, Alice, who gave him his unusual name because she and her future husband had first met at a picnic on the shores of Lake Rudyard in Staffordshire, accompanied her bridegroom out to India when Lockwood accepted the post of Professor of Architectural Sculpture at a new school of Art in Bombay. And it was in this city that their son, 'Ruddy' or 'Rud' to his family and friends, was born on December 30th 1865. Like the great majority of Anglo-Indian children he enjoyed an idyllic childhood. I use the term Anglo-Indian in its original sense. It was coined to describe the British who spent their working lives in India and returned to their own country on retirement, and it did not mean as it does now, people of mixed blood. Both Kipling's parents and mine would have described themselves as Anglo-Indians.

Indians are endlessly kind and tolerant towards small children, and Ruddy was never to forget his bearer, Meeta, or the colour and clamour of the bazaars, the sound of the night wind through palm and banana leaves, or the 'far-going Arab dhows on the pearly water and gaily dressed Parsees wading out to worship the sun'. He was six when those halcyon days ended abruptly. His parents took him and his little sister, Trix, home to England where, without a word of warning or explanation, they left them in a narrow, chilly house in a street of similar houses in Southsea in the care of a narrow-minded woman who eked out her husband's pension by fostering the children of Anglo-Indians. They were not to see their parents again for six long, unhappy years.

Trix, a pretty and endearing three-year-old too young to be greatly affected by the parting, became something of a household pet. But poor, betrayed Ruddy was to bear the scars of those six bleak years for the rest of his life. The woman that he was told to call 'Auntie' Rosa (it being a tiresome Victorian convention that children should regard their parents adult friends and acquaintances as 'Aunties' and 'Uncles') systematically ill-treated him; punishing him for every fault, real or imagined, and allowing her teenage son to bully him unmercifully. Long afterwards he was to write his own account of those bitter years in a harrowing short story entitled *Baa, Baa, Black Sheep,* and according to that, when 'Auntie Rosa' discovered that he had a passion for books, she took to punishing him by forbidding him to read — with the result that he read in secret; by firelight, the flame of a filched candle-end or in the dusk; thereby straining his eyes to a point where he could see nothing that was not a few inches away from his nose. When his work shows patches of crassness and cruelty, it might be as well for his critics to remember that he served a grim apprenticeship to life. And also that he too could plead an excuse that is trotted out nowadays to condone almost any crime, however appalling, committed by some vicious yobbo: that he/she was 'the victim of a deprived childhood' and should therefore be treated leniently.

The only wells in the lonely child's desert of misery were the annual December holidays spent with Aunt Georgie and Uncle Ned Burne-Jones at their house in London's North End Road: The Grange. And when, many years later, he heard that The Grange was to be pulled down, he begged for the iron bell-pull that hung by the front door, because he wanted to hang it by his own, in the hope that other children would in the future pull it with as much excitement and anticipation as he had done in the past. It hangs there to this day by the front door of Batemans, his house in Sussex, and since my own house was not far from his, which can now be visited because it belongs to the National Trust, I used to go there fairly often, and every time I passed that bell-pull I would touch it: just to show him that people still remembered, and cared about him.

In the end it was Aunt Georgie who wrote a letter to her sister that brought Alice hurrying back from India, to find her once boistrous and talkative little son half blind and as wary, silent and suspicious as a wild animal that has been caged and ill-treated. It says a lot for Alice Kipling's charm that despite the six years of purgatory to which she had doomed him, she managed to lure him back to her in a very short time, and that he remained devoted to her and to Lockwood all his days. Yet as he himself was to write, 'when young lips have drunk deep of the bitter waters of Hate, Suspicion and Despair, all the Love in the world will not wholly take away that knowledge'.

One of the worst results of those six years in Southsea was that for the rest of his life he had to wear the thick lensed spectacles that led to his being nicknamed 'Gig-lamps,' or 'Gigger' at school, the United Services College at Westward Ho! in Devon. The school was Anglo-Indian by tradition and specialised in getting its pupils through the Army Exams, but

FOREWORD

'Gigger's' poor sight would have debarred him from the army if he had wished to enter it; which he did not. Fortunately for him, the College had an original type of Headmaster who encouraged his reading and by appointing him editor of the College magazine, hooked him for life on journalism and printer's ink. One can see the shape of things to come when, having been punished for failing to do his homework on an *Ode by Horace*[1], the future winner of the Nobel Prize for Literature handed in a translation done in broad Devonshire dialect:

> He– 'So long as 'twaz me alone
>   An' there wasn't no other chaps,
>   I was praoud as a king on 'is throne –
>   Happier tu per'aps.'
>
> She– 'So long as 'twaz only I
>   An' there wasn't no other she
>   Yeou cared for so much –
>   Shurely – I was glad as glad could be.'
>
> He– 'But now I'm in lovv with Jane Pritt –
>   She can play the piano, she can;
>   An' if dyin' 'ud 'elp 'er a bit
>   I'd die laike a man.'
>
> She– 'You'm like me. I'm in lovv with Frye –
>   Him as lives out tu Appledore Quay;
>   An' if dyin' 'ud 'elp 'im I'd die –
>   Twice ovver for he.'
>
> He– 'But s'posin' I threwed up Jane
>   An' niver went walking with she –
>   An' come back to yeou again –
>   How' ud that be?'
>
> She– 'Frye's sober. 'Yeou've allus done badly –
>   An' yeou shifts like cut net floats, yeou do:
>   But – I'd throw that young Frye over gladly
>   An' lovv 'ee right thru!'

Not bad for a fifteen-year-old!

In a novel based on his schooldays called *Stalky and Co,* that shocked the critics into denouncing its three schoolboy heroes as 'little beasts', there is a touching account of the sixteen-year-old Ruddy, in the character of 'Beetle' at the end of his last term, rushing breathless and white with excitement to his study-mates, Stalky and McTurk, to tell them the wonderful news that he is to sail for India, passage paid, where there is a job waiting for him as Assistant Editor of a newspaper, at the magnificent salary of £100 a year!

1. *Donec gratus eram tibi* — in case anyone with a classical education is interested.

That would have been in the summer of 1882. And well over half a century later, in the same year that he died, I happened to be on a motor tour through Devon with a schoolfriend whose parents had lent us their car. Stopping at Westward Ho! on a cloudless afternoon we went down to the shore to sit on the Pebble Ridge, and looking out towards Lundy Island I thought of the boy Ruddy, 'walking high and disposedly round the wreck of a Spanish galleon, shouting and declaiming against the long ridged seas.' There were no long-ridged waves that day, for the sea was satin smooth. But I knew that the view I was looking at could not have changed at all since that young Rudyard, with all his adult life still ahead of him, had sat where I was sitting and day-dreamed about the future — not knowing that he would one day be one of the immortals. And now it was all over. He was dead and his story had ended, and it occurred to me for the first time that life, which until then had seemed very long, was in reality dauntingly short, and that it behoved me to make the very most of every minute of it. To 'fill the unforgiving minute with sixty seconds' worth of distance run', in fact. Which is something I have done ever since, so that I can honestly say, like Rudyard's Tramp Royal, 'So write, before I die, "She liked it all"'[2].

That job as assistant editor may have sounded impressive, but in practice it turned out to consist of at least half-a-dozen jobs, and young Ruddy found himself working like a galley-slave as compositor, reporter, journalist and general handy-man. When there was not enough material to complete a page, he could write short pieces, either verses or stories, to fill in the gaps. These 'fill-ins' caught the public's fancy and became very popular with regular readers — among them my father, who had arrived out in India a bit later than Ruddy. He was so taken with them that he took to cutting them out and keeping them, long before he knew who had written them or even if they were all different. The first appearances of *Pagett, MP* for instance, was signed 'An Englishman'.

Lahore is not a pleasant place to spend the hot weather, and the *Civil and Military Gazette*'s youthful assistant editor suffered all the ills of the season, aggravated by the insomnia which was to plague him all his life. Unable to sleep, he took to spending his heat-tormented nights wandering through the streets and alleyways of the walled city. And here I would like to point out to certain of his biographers who have skimped their research, that it was Lahore, and *not* Calcutta that he dubbed 'The City of Dreadful Night'!

My father — who for some long forgotten reason I called Tacklow — told me a nice story about the young Ruddy's early years in Lahore. It had been told to him by a senior Anglo-Indian who had been stationed there for years, to whom Tacklow had mentioned a fill-in that had appeared in that morning's edition of the *Civil and Military Gazette*. The elderly civilian had said: 'Probably by that young feller who's assistant editor — name of Kipling. We'll be hearing a lot more about him one of these days, mark my words! Extraordinary youth! He not only seems to be on first-name terms with every Khan, Singh and Hurree in the bazaars, but I've seen him with my own eyes squatting on his hunkers like

2. For 'She' read 'E' — *Sestina of the Tramp Royal*.

a coolie and chatting man-to-man with a *Sadhu* of all people! — one of those holy bolies who would consider his food polluted and throw it all away if your shadow or mine happened to fall across it. Amazing!'

I have learned since that a good many people noted the young Kipling's ability to get anyone to talk to him, and I have no doubt that all his stories were based on tales he got from strangers or chance acquaintances. Tacklow said that most of the Simla stories certainly were, and that Kipling, who had been allowed to take hot-weather leave in Simla after that first year, had gained much of his information by reserving one particular table in the dining-room of a Club, from where it was possible, due to some quirk of the acoustics, to hear everything that was said at certain tables in the other half of the room, and thus listen-in to all the gossip of the station. Affronted members who found their most secret goings-on turned into short stories in the *Civil and Military Gazette* (and later published in *Plain Tales from the Hills* and *Under the Deodars*) were, said Tacklow, simply furious and declared *Civil and Military Gazette*'s assistant editor to be a cad and a bounder. Nor were they amused when the bounder in question actually had the audacity to disclose the method by which he had acquired his information; kindly explaining it in detail in a short story called *The Bisara of Pooree*. After that the committee hastily ordered the dining-room to be re-designed, and its peculiar acoustics vanished.

It is strange, when you come to think of it, that Kipling's name should be so firmly linked with India when, apart from his earliest childhood and a couple of extremely brief visits in later life, he only spent six and a half years in that country, and when he left it early in 1889, can be said to have left it for good. So what happened after that? Well, practically everything. All his best work, for a start. Fame and fortune, and more than his fair share of tragedy. But as almost everyone within sight has written a book about him, anyone who is interested can easily find out. For myself, I like to remember that he loved his country dearly, and though he frequently criticised her, his best girl from first to last was Britannia, to whom he remained faithful to the end.

When he died his ashes were interred in Westminster Abbey. Which I suppose was only appropriate. But he wrote some verses in *Puck of Pook's Hill* that suggest he would have preferred to be buried in his beloved Sussex. Here are the last two lines of the last verse of *A Three-Part Song*:

'Oh, Firle an' Ditchling an' sails at sea,
I reckon you keep my soul for me!'

I reckon they do, Rud.

M·M·KAYE
The Old House
East Sussex
Jan 26th 1987

'THE LAST SUTTEE'

Part One

—

EAST OF SUEZ

PRELUDE
To 'Departmental Ditties'

I have eaten your bread and salt.
*   I have drunk your water and wine.*
The deaths ye died I have watched beside,
*   And the lives ye led were mine.*

Was there aught that I did not share
*   In vigil or toil or ease,—*
One joy or woe that I did not know,
*   Dear hearts across the seas?*

I have written the tale of our life
*   For a sheltered people's mirth,*
In jesting guise—but ye are wise,
*   And ye know what the jest is worth.*

This is the Anglo-Indian speaking
to his fellow Anglo-Indians for
whose entertainment he has written
these verses and stories.
The 'sheltered' people are the stay-at-
home British who will laugh or gasp
or be shocked, but will not understand
what is true or what is satire, and
what lies under them.

THE MOON
OF OTHER DAYS

Beneath the deep verandah's shade,
  When bats begin to fly,
I sit me down and watch—alas!
  Another evening die.
Blood-red behind the sere *ferash*[1]
  She rises through the haze.
Sainted Diana! can that be
  The Moon of Other Days?

Ah! shade of little Kitty Smith,
  Sweet Saint of Kensington!
Say, was it ever thus at Home
  The Moon of August shone,
When arm in arm we wandered long
  Through Putney's evening haze,
And Hammersmith was Heaven beneath
  The Moon of Other Days?

But Wandle's stream is Sutlej now,
  And Putney's evening haze
The dust that half a hundred kine
  Before my window raise.
Unkempt, unclean, athwart the mist
  The seething city looms,
In place of Putney's golden gorse
  The sickly *babul*[2] blooms.

Glare down, old Hecate, through the dust,
  And bid the pie-dog yell,
Draw from the drain its typhoid-germ,
  From each bazar its smell;
Yea, suck the fever from the tank
  And sap my strength therewith:
Thank Heaven, you show a smiling face
  To little Kitty Smith!

[1]Tamarisk [2]Acacia

[3]

I love this early poem for its description of late evening and nightfall in the plains of India. In the hot weather before the monsoon breaks, a full moon rising in the dusty twilight is red—and enormous: more like a sun setting than a moon rising! That's because of the dust that, in Kipling's day, was raised by 'half a hundred kine' and in the present one by taxis, lorries, buses and bicycles. The Kitty Smith of these verses is obviously Rudyard's lost love Flo Garrard who was also the heroine of his first novel 'The Light that failed.'

I can sympathise with young Rudyard in his first hot-weather in Lahore, looking up at a glaring Indian moon and thinking of other moonlight nights. Because to this day I never see a full moon without thinking that only a few hours ago it was shining down on the Dal Lake and Chashmashai; and on any number of other places that I loved and was happy in. And always it seemed impossible that this can be so; and that they are still there! Which sounds a bit like Ronald Knox's famous limerick: "There once was a man who said God / Must think it exceedingly odd / If He finds that this tree continues to be / When there's no one about in the Quad."

To which some anonymous genius wrote the following reply: "Dear Sir, your astonishment's odd: I am always about in the Quad. / And that's why the tree continues to be / Since observed by, Yours faithfully God". It's a comforting thought—that He will always be observing all the lovely and lovingly-remembered places in his lovely world!

This was written in 1886 at a time when The Empire was celebrating Queen Victoria's Golden Jubilee. A *tamarsha* (festivity) that would have meant nothing at all to the thrifty, hard-working and philosophical peasants of rural India — apart from the fact that any *tamarsha*, particularly one accompanied by fireworks was always a welcome break in the monotony of daily life.

I do not know how it is with villages in these very different times. But in Kipling's day and even in mine, They cared little for Governments or politics; for they had other and more important things to think about. Births, deaths and marriages; and above all the weather, upon which the crops, and their lives depended. And provided that they paid their taxes, which were remitted in bad years, the Government interferred with them as little as possible. Which I suppose is why Mahatma Gandhi regarded village life as the ideal and hoped to make all India live in rural peace and simplicity.

WHAT THE PEOPLE SAID

By the well, where the bullocks go
Silent and blind and slow—
By the field, where the young corn dies
In the face of the sultry skies,
They have heard, as the dull earth hears
The voice of the wind of an hour,
The sound of the Great Queen's voice:—
'My God hath given me years,
'Hath granted dominion and power:
'And I bid you, O Land, rejoice.'

And the Ploughman settles the share
More deep in the grudging clod;
For he saith:—'The wheat is my care,
'And the rest is the will of God.
'He sent the Mahratta spear
'As he sendeth the rain,
'And the *Mlech*,[1] in the fated year,
'Broke the spear in twain,
'And was broken in turn. Who knows
'How our Lords make strife?
'It is good that the young wheat grows,
'For the bread is Life.'

Then, far and near, as the twilight drew,
    Hissed up to the scornful dark
Great serpents, blazing, of red and blue,
That rose and faded, and rose anew,
    That the Land might wonder and mark.
'To-day is a day of days,' they said,
'Make merry, O People, all!'
And the Ploughman listened and bowed his head.
'To-day and to-morrow God's will,' he said,
    As he trimmed the lamps on the wall.

[1] The foreigner

[4]

'He sendeth us years that are good,
'As He sendeth the dearth.
'He giveth to each man his food,
'Or Her food to the Earth.
'Our Kings and our Queens are afar—
'On their peoples be peace—
'God bringeth the rain to the Bar,
'That our cattle increase.'

And the Ploughman settled the share
More deep in the sun-dried clod:—
'Mogul, Mahratta, and *Mlech* from the North,
'And White Queen over the Seas—
'God raiseth them up and driveth them forth
'As the dust of the ploughshare flies in the breeze;
'But the wheat and the cattle are all my care,
'And the rest is the will of God.'

There is a story, not entirely apocryphal, that nicely illustrates the remoteness of many of India's villages. It tells of a party of political activists who, in 1947 when the date of Independence had been set and was fast approaching, arrived at a small village in the middle of nowhere and told the villagers to hang out flags and decorate their houses in celebration of the Great Day. The villagers were politely interested. "Yes, yes assuredly they would do so; but what Great Day?" What were they celebrating?"
"Freedom!"
"Freedom?— freedom from what?"
"From the British of course! The British are going!"
The village elders looked puzzled and finally one of them said:
"We didn't know that they had come."
The chances are that they didn't!

[5]

THE LAST SUTTEE

Not many years ago a King died in one of the Rajpoot States. His wives, disregarding the orders of the English against Suttee, would have broken out of the palace and burned themselves with the corpse, had not the gates been barred. But one of them, disguised as the King's favourite dancing girl, passed through the line of guards and reached the pyre. There, her courage failing, she prayed her cousin, a baron of the King's court, to kill her. This he did, not knowing who she was.

This is another true story, and you can find an account of it in the first volume of R.K's 'From Sea to Sea' The King in these verses was a Maharajrana of Udaipur. But this was by no means the 'last suttee'. There have been many more since then — notably one that took place in Jodhpur in 1967, and which I was told about in some detail by a neice of the suttee. The British outlawed the burning of widows over a century and a half ago. But India is a vast country and it proved impossible to police all of it. Widows continued to burn. And still do. Though now in very small numbers. But the rite is still considered holy.

Udai Chand lay sick to death
   In his hold by Gungra hill.
All night we heard the death-gongs ring,
For the soul of the dying Rajpoot King,
All night beat up from the women's wing
   A cry that we could not still.

All night the barons came and went,
   The Lords of the Outer Guard.
All night the cressets glimmered pale
On Ulwar sabre and Tonk jezail,
Mewar headstall and Marwar mail,
   That clinked in the palace yard.

In the Golden Room on the palace roof
   All night he fought for air;
And there were sobbings behind the screen,
Rustle and whisper of women unseen,
And the hungry eyes of the Boondi Queen
   On the death she might not share.

He passed at dawn—the death-fire leaped
   From ridge to river-head,
From the Malwa plains to the Abu scars:
And wail upon wail went up to the stars
Behind the grim zenana-bars,
   When they knew that the King was dead.

[6]

The dumb priest knelt to tie his mouth
  And robe him for the pyre.
The Boondi Queen beneath us cried:
'See, now, that we die as our mothers died
'In the bridal-bed by our master's side!
  'Out, women!—to the fire!'

We drove the great gates home apace—
  White hands were on the sill—
But ere the rush of the unseen feet
Had reached the turn to the open street,
The bars shot down, the guard-drum beat—
  We held the dovecot still!

A face looked down in the gathering day,
  And laughing spoke from the wall:
'Ohé, they mourn here: let me by—
'Azizun, the Lucknow nautch-girl, I!
'When the house is rotten, the rats must fly,
  'And I seek another thrall.

'For I ruled the King as ne'er did Queen,—
  'To-night the Queens rule me!
'Guard them safely, but let me go,
'Or ever they pay the debt they owe
'In scourge and torture!' She leaped below,
  And the grim guard watched her flee.

They knew that the King had spent his soul
  On a North-bred dancing-girl:
That he prayed to a flat-nosed Lucknow god,
And kissed the ground where her feet had trod,
And doomed to death at her drunken nod,
  And swore by her lightest curl.

We bore the King to his fathers' place,
  Where the tombs of the Sun-born stand:
Where the grey apes swing, and the peacocks preen
On fretted pillar and jewelled screen,
And the wild boar couch in the house of the Queen
  On the drift of the desert sand.

The herald read his titles forth
  We set the logs aglow:
'Friend of the English, free from fear,
'Baron of Luni to Jeysulmeer,
'Lord of the Desert of Bikaneer,
  'King of the Jungle,—go!'

All night the red flame stabbed the sky
  With wavering wind-tossed spears:
And out of a shattered temple crept
A woman who veiled her head and wept,
And called on the King—but the great King slept,
  And turned not for her tears.

One watched, a bow-shot from the blaze,
  The silent streets between,
Who had stood by the King in sport and fray,
To blade in ambush or boar at bay,
And he was a baron old and grey,
  And kin to the Boondi Queen.

Small thought had he to mark the strife—
  Cold fear with hot desire—
When thrice she leaped from the leaping flame,
And thrice she beat her breast for shame,
And thrice like a wounded dove she came
  And moaned about the fire.

He said: 'O shameless, put aside
   'The veil upon thy brow!
'Who held the King and all his land
'To the wanton will of a harlot's hand!
'Will the white ash rise from the blistered brand?
   Stoop down and call him now!'

Then she: 'By the faith of my tarnished soul,
   'All things I did not well
'I had hoped to clear ere the fire died,
'And lay me down by my master's side
'To rule in Heaven his only bride,
   'While the others howl in Hell.

'But I have felt the fire's breath,
   'And hard it is to die!
'Yet if I may pray a Rajpoot lord
'To sully the steel of a Thakur's sword
'With base-born blood of a trade abhorred...'
   And the Thakur answered, 'Ay.'

He drew and struck: the straight blade drank
   The life beneath the breast.
'I had looked for the Queen to face the flame,
'But the harlot dies for the Rajpoot dame—
'Sister of mine, pass, free from shame.
   'Pass with thy King to rest!'

The black log crashed above the white:
   The little flames and lean,
Red as slaughter and blue as steel,
That whistled and fluttered from head to heel,
Leaped up anew, for they found their meal
   On the heart of—the Boondi Queen!

ARITHMETIC
ON THE FRONTIER

A great and glorious thing it is
　　To learn, for seven years or so,
The Lord knows what of that and this,
　　Ere reckoned fit to face the foe—
The flying bullet down the Pass,
That whistles clear: 'All flesh is grass.'

Three hundred pounds per annum spent
　　On making brain and body meeter
For all the murderous intent
　　Comprised in 'villainous saltpetre'!
And after?—Ask the Yusufzaies
What comes of all our 'ologies.

A scrimmage in a Border Station—
　　A canter down some dark defile—
Two thousand pounds of education
　　Drops to a ten-rupee jezail—
The Crammer's boast, the Squadron's pride,
Shot like a rabbit in a ride!

No proposition Euclid wrote
　　No formulæ the text-books know,
Will turn the bullet from your coat,
　　Or ward the tulwar's downward blow.
Strike hard who cares—shoot straight who can—
The odds are on the cheaper man.

One sword-knot stolen from the camp
　　Will pay for all the school expenses
Of any Kurrum Valley scamp
　　Who knows no word of moods and tenses,
But, being blessed with perfect sight,
Picks off our messmates left and right.

That 'flying bullet down the Pass' took a yearly toll of the young British Army officers who served in Indian regiments right up to the day of Independence and Partition. The Yusufzai were only one of the border tribes who waged perpetual warfare against Britain's Indian Army.

I wonder what the present day equivalent of that £300 is? —£3000—£10,000? Or more?

Our last-but-one Army posting in India (it was still India then, for Pakistan had yet to be born) was in a lonely fort in the Kurrum Valley which, at that time, was tribal territory. I suppose that is why Kipling speaks of a 'Kurrum Valley scamp', because the tribesmen were no respectors of the law.

With home-bred hordes the hillsides teem.
  The troopships bring us one by one,
At vast expense of time and steam,
  To slay Afridis where they run.
The 'captives of our bow and spear'
Are cheap, alas! as we are dear.

This last verse remained true to the end of the 'Raj'! And still does —as the Russians will undoubtedly find out! The hills of the North West Frontier will always teem with home-bred hordes of Afridi tribesmen ready to repel boarders. As in Kiplings day —and mine.

Shiv, Shiva The Cosmic dancer, is The oldest and perhaps The greatest of The gods in The Hindu pantheon; and this is one of the many folk-tales—and The nicest, I think—That are told about him. He is not only The Preserver, but the Destroyer; and one of his names is Mahadeo.

His wife, The beautiful Pavati, is also Durga the Goddess of Smallpox; Kali the terrible, drinker of blood; and Mother of The Universe, Uma. But in This story she is merely Pavati, The teasing wife playing a trick on her husband.

Shiv, who poured the harvest and made the winds to blow,
Sitting at the doorways of a day of long ago,
Gave to each his portion, food and toil and fate,
From the King upon the *guddee*[1] to the Beggar at the gate.
   All things made he—Shiva the Preserver.
   Mahadeo! Mahadeo! He made all,—
   Thorn for the camel, fodder for the kine,
   And Mother's heart for sleepy head, O little Son of mine!

Wheat he gave to rich folk, millet to the poor,
Broken scraps for holy men that beg from door to door;
Cattle to the tiger, carrion to the kite,
And rags and bones to wicked wolves without the wall at night.
Naught he found too lofty, none he saw too low—
Parbati beside him watched them come and go;
Thought to cheat her husband, turning Shiv to jest—
Stole the little grasshopper and hid it in her breast.
   So she tricked him, Shiva the Preserver.
   Mahadeo! Mahadeo, turn and see!
   Tall are the camels, heavy are the kine,
   But this was Least of Little Things, O little Son of mine!

When the dole was ended, laughingly she said,
'Master, of a million mouths is not one unfed?'
Laughing, Shiv made answer, 'All have had their part,
Even he, the little one, hidden 'neath thy heart.'
From her breast she plucked it, Parbati the thief,
Saw the Least of Little Things gnawed a new-grown leaf!
Saw and feared and wondered, making prayer to Shiv,
Who hath surely given meat to all that live!
   All things made he—Shiva the Preserver.
   Mahadeo! Mahadeo! He made all,—
   Thorn for the camel, fodder for the kine,
   And Mother's heart for sleepy head, O little Son of mine!

[1] Throne

[12]

THE HYÆNAS

After the burial-parties leave
    And the baffled kites have fled;
The wise hyænas come out at eve
    To take account of our dead.

How he died and why he died
    Troubles them not a whit.
They snout the bushes and stones aside
    And dig till they come to it.

They are only resolute they shall eat
    That they and their mates may thrive,
And they know that the dead are safer meat
    Than the weakest thing alive.

(For a goat may butt, and a worm may sting,
    And a child will sometimes stand;
But a poor dead soldier of the King
    Can never lift a hand.)

They whoop and halloo and scatter the dirt
    Until their tushes white
Take good hold of the Army shirt,
    And tug the corpse to light,

And the pitiful face is shewn again
    For an instant ere they close;
But it is not discovered to living men—
    Only to God and to those

Who, being soulless, are free from shame,
    Whatever meat they may find.
Nor do they defile the dead man's name—
    That is reserved for his kind.

It is hard to believe that even its mother could love a hyæna, for they really are revolting creatures.
They manage to look deformed—a sort of animal version of the Hunchback of Notre Dame—and to sound like a gaggle of hysterical fiends.
They sneak and cringe and steal and nothing is too horrible for them to eat. But they eat to live. And there are occasions when homo-sapiens can be a great deal nastier and more hideously cruel.

THE BALLAD OF EAST AND WEST

*Oh, East is East, and West is West, and never the twain
        shall meet,*
*Till Earth and Sky stand presently at God's great Judgment
        Seat;*
*But there is neither East nor West, Border, nor Breed, nor
        Birth,*
*When two strong men stand face to face, though they come
        from the ends of the earth!*

Kamal is out with twenty men to raise the Border-side,
And he has lifted the Colonel's mare that is the Colonel's
        pride.
He has lifted her out of the stable-door between the dawn
        and the day,
And turned the calkins upon her feet, and ridden her far
        away.
Then up and spoke the Colonel's son that led a troop of the
        Guides:
'Is there never a man of all my men can say where Kamal
        hides?'
Then up and spoke Mohammed Khan, the son of the
        Ressaldar:
'If ye know the track of the morning-mist, ye know where
        his pickets are.
'At dusk he harries the Abazai—at dawn he is into Bonair,
'But he must go by Fort Bukloh to his own place to fare.
'So if ye gallop to Fort Bukloh as fast as a bird can fly,
'By the favour of God ye may cut him off ere he win to the
        Tongue of Jagai.
'But if he be past the Tongue of Jagai, right swiftly turn ye
        then,
'For the length and the breadth of that grisly plain is sown
        with Kamal's men.
'There is rock to the left, and rock to the right, and low
        lean thorn between,

[14]

'And ye may hear a breech-bolt snick where never a man
    is seen.'
The Colonel's son has taken horse, and a raw rough dun
    was he,
With the mouth of a bell and the heart of Hell and the head
    of a gallows-tree.
The Colonel's son to the Fort has won, they bid him stay
    to eat—
Who rides at the tail of a Border thief, he sits not long at
    his meat.
He's up and away from Fort Bukloh as fast as he can fly,
Till he was aware of his father's mare in the gut of the
    Tongue of Jagai,
Till he was aware of his father's mare with Kamal upon her
    back,
And when he could spy the white of her eye, he made the
    pistol crack.
He has fired once, he has fired twice, but the whistling ball
    went wide.
'Ye shoot like a soldier,' Kamal said. 'Show now if ye can
    ride!'
It's up and over the Tongue of Jagai, as blown dust-devils
    go,
The dun he fled like a stag of ten, but the mare like a
    barren doe,
The dun he leaned against the bit and slugged his head
    above,
But the red mare played with the snaffle-bars, as a maiden
    plays with a glove.
There was rock to the left and rock to the right, and low
    lean thorn between,
And thrice he heard a breech-bolt snick tho' never a man
    was seen.
They have ridden the low moon out of the sky, their hoofs
    drum up the dawn,
The dun he went like a wounded bull, but the mare like a
    new-roused fawn.

[15]

Most of the verses in
this book have been
chosen for reasons
that have nothing to
do with their literary
merit.
This ballad, for
instance, was chosen
for a strictly
sentimental one:
because my husband,
Goff Hamilton,
served in The Guides-
the third of his
name to do so. The
first being the
Walter Pollack Hamilton,
V.C, who I used as
a character in a
novel called The Far
Pavilions, and who
died in 1879 in the
defence of the British
Residency in Kabul,
together with the
Envoy and his staff
and seventy-one
members of an eighty-
strong escort of Guides.
The second, Colonel
Bill Hamilton, was
my father-in-law,
and the third and
last, was Goff.

This is — or was — still true of the Frontier, for any Pathan worth his salt seemed to be able to conceal himself behind half a brick. Though that does not help them much nowadays. Not long ago, when Goff and I were re-visiting the Khyber, an indignant tribesman complained to Goff that the Russians were no gentlemen — "In the old days" he said "Things were very different. You could climb, we could climb. You had guns, we had guns. We understood each other. But these Russ-log come sneaking round the top of our hills in helicopter gun-ships that blow fire on us that can even follow us into caves and behind rocks!" He plainly considered this to be a most unsportsmanlike tactic. Though he did admit that "They are like us. If we catch of of them we kill him — slowly. And they do the like. You did not do that —" There was a slight suggestion of scorn in the last remark!

The dun he fell at a water-course—in a woeful heap fell he,
And Kamal has turned the red mare back, and pulled the rider free.
He has knocked the pistol out of his hand—small room was there to strive,
'"Twas only by favour of mine,' quoth he, 'ye rode so long alive:
'There was not a rock for twenty mile, there was not a clump of tree,
'But covered a man of my own men with a rifle cocked on his knee.
'If I had raised my bridle-hand, as I have held it low,
'The little jackals that flee so fast were feasting all in a row.
'If I had bowed my head on my breast, as I have held it high,
'The kite that whistles above us now were gorged till she could not fly.'
Lightly answered the Colonel's son: 'Do good to bird and beast,
'But count who come for the broken meats before thou makest a feast.
'If there should follow a thousand swords to carry my bones away,
'Belike the price of a jackal's meal were more than a thief could pay.
'They will feed their horse on the standing crop, their men on the garnered grain.
'The thatch of the byres will serve their fires when all the cattle are slain.
'But if thou thinkest the price be fair,—thy brethren wait to sup,
'The hound is kin to the jackal-spawn,—howl, dog, and call them up!
'And if thou thinkest the price be high, in steer and gear and stack,

[16]

'Give me my father's mare again, and I'll fight my own way
        back!'
Kamal has gripped him by the hand and set him upon his
        feet.
'No talk shall be of dogs,' said he, 'when wolf and grey
        wolf meet.
'May I eat dirt if thou has hurt of me in deed or breath;
'What dam of lances brought thee forth to jest at the dawn
        with Death?'
Lightly answered the Colonel's son: 'I hold by the blood of
        my clan:
'Take up the mare for my father's gift—by God, she has
        carried a man!'
The red mare ran to the Colonel's son, and nuzzled against
        his breast;
'We be two strong men,' said Kamal then, 'but she loveth
        the younger best.

'Lightly answered the
Colonel's son: "I hold by
the blood of my clan: ...."

'So she shall go with a lifter's dower, my turquoise-
        studded rein,
'My 'broidered saddle and saddle-cloth, and silver stirrups
        twain.'
The Colonel's son a pistol drew, and held it muzzle-end,
'Ye have taken the one from a foe,' said he. 'Will ye take
        the mate from a friend?'
'A gift for a gift,' said Kamal straight; 'a limb for the risk of
        a limb.
'Thy father has sent his son to me, I'll send my son to
        him!'
With that he whistled his only son, that dropped from a
        mountain-crest—
He trod the ling like a buck in spring, and he looked like a
        lance in rest.
'Now here is thy master,' Kamal said, 'who leads a troop
        of the Guides,
'And thou must ride at his left side as shield on shoulder
        rides.

Kamal's son was by no means the only Border bandit to join the Guides in an unorthodox manner, for one of the Corps most-famous members was a notorious brigand by the name of Dilawur Khan, who the Commanding-Officer, probably half in jest, invited to join the Guides. Dilawur apparently laughed his head off, but to everyone's surprise, accepted. He rose to be a non-commissioned officer and died a hero's death.

Another was Bahaud-din Khan a member of the Kazilbash Horse that broke and ran in an action against the Guides during the opening stages of the Second Afghan War. He was so disgusted by his country-mens cowardly behaviour that he offered his sword to the enemy on the spot, and served with the Guides for the rest of the campaign—only leaving them when peace broke out two years later. Because, he said, the prospect of peace-time soldiering in a military cantonment was too boring to be borne. He preferred to return to his own country—"The land of never-ending conflict."

'Till Death or I cut loose the tie, at camp and board and bed,
'Thy life is his—thy fate it is to guard him with thy head.
'So, thou must eat the White Queen's meat, and all her foes are thine,
'And thou must harry thy father's hold for the peace of the Border-line.
'And thou must make a trooper tough and hack thy way to power—
'Belike they will raise thee to Ressaldar when I am hanged at Peshawur!'

They have looked each other between the eyes, and there they found no fault.
They have taken the Oath of the Brother-in-Blood on leavened bread and salt:
They have taken the Oath of the Brother-in-Blood on fire and fresh-cut sod,
On the hilt and the haft of the Khyber knife, and the Wondrous Names of God.
The Colonel's son he rides the mare and Kamal's boy the dun,
And two have come back to Fort Bukloh where there went forth but one.
And when they drew to the Quarter-Guard, full twenty swords flew clear—
There was not a man but carried his feud with the blood of the mountaineer.
'Ha' done! ha' done!' said the Colonel's son. 'Put up the steel at your sides!
'Last night ye had struck at a Border thief—to-night 'tis a man of the Guides!'

*Oh, East is East, and West is West, and never the twain
  shall meet,
Till Earth and Sky stand presently at God's great Judgment
  Seat;
But there is neither East nor West, Border, nor Breed, nor
  Birth,
When two strong men stand face to face, though they come
  from the ends of the earth!*

I put Bahaud-din's story into the original draft of The Far Pavilions, but like many other fascinating stories of the Guides and the frontier, my publishers, horrified at the size of that book, cut it out. One sees their point!

The drawing on this page is a sketch of the silver statuette of Wally Hamilton V.C., fighting his last fight in the outer courtyard of the burning Residency in Kabul. It is a copy of the original life size statue (now in the National Army Museum in London), and it stands today in the Guides Mess, in Pakistan, where I am happy to say the Guides are still going strong!

'Ford O' Kabul River'

People tend to think of events that took place 'way back in the 19th century as being so far away. They have become History. And History, as everyone knows, is in the remote past—Henry the Eighth and all that! But very often you only have to glance over your shoulder to find that it is, in fact, just behind you — so close that you could almost reach out and touch it. For instance, I myself lived well into Kipling's day; yet he wrote this lament only a few years after the tragedy that it commemorates, and was a schoolboy of thirteen when it happened — not all that much younger than some of the troopers who were drowned in the river that night.

My father, who was three years Kipling's junior, remembered a shocked grown-up reading the news of the tragedy out loud from the pages of some daily newspaper. The Morning Post perhaps?

FORD O' KABUL RIVER

Kabul town's by Kabul river—
  Blow the trumpet, draw the sword—
There I lef' my mate for ever,
  Wet an' drippin' by the ford.
    Ford, ford, ford o' Kabul river,
      Ford o' Kabul river in the dark!
    There's the river up and brimmin', an' there's
      'arf a squadron swimmin'
    'Cross the ford o' Kabul river in the dark.

Kabul town's a blasted place—
  Blow the trumpet, draw the sword—
'Strewth I shan't forget 'is face
  Wet an' drippin' by the ford!
    Ford, ford, ford o' Kabul river,
      Ford o' Kabul river in the dark!
    Keep the crossing-stakes beside you, an' they will
      surely guide you
    'Cross the ford o' Kabul river in the dark.

Kabul town is sun and dust—
  Blow the trumpet, draw the sword—
I'd ha' sooner drownded fust
  'Stead of 'im beside the ford.
    Ford, ford, ford o' Kabul river,
      Ford o' Kabul river in the dark!
    You can 'ear the 'orses threshin'; you can 'ear
      the men a-splashin',
    'Cross the ford o' Kabul river in the dark.

I don't know when this lament for drowned soldiers was first put to music, but I know we used to sing it to a piano during the school holidays at the home of a school-friend of my father's. It had a most haunting tune and here is a fragment of the refrain—

Kabul town was ours to take—
    Blow the trumpet, draw the sword—
I'd ha' left it for 'is sake—
    'Im that left me by the ford.
        Ford, ford, ford o' Kabul river,
            Ford o' Kabul river in the dark!
        It's none so bloomin' dry there; ain't you never
            comin' nigh there,
                'Cross the ford o' Kabul river in the dark?

Kabul town'll go to hell—
    Blow the trumpet, draw the sword—
'Fore I see him 'live an' well—
    'Im the best beside the ford.
        Ford, ford, ford o' Kabul river,
            Ford o' Kabul river in the dark!
        Gawd 'elp 'em if they blunder, for their boots'll
            pull 'em under,
                By the ford o' Kabul river in the dark.

Turn your 'orse from Kabul town—
    Blow the trumpet, draw the sword—
'Im an' 'arf my troop is down,
    Down and drownded by the ford.
        Ford, ford, ford o' Kabul river,
            Ford o' Kabul river in the dark!
        There's the river low an' fallin', but it ain't no use
            a-callin'
                'Cross the ford o' Kabul river in the dark!

Back in The 18th century
Kabul was spelt Car-bool.
And in Kipling's day
and my father's, right down
to my own, it was spelt
Kabul and pronounced
Kor-bul: The A, for some
reason being OR. (Listen
to a frontier tribesman
saying it! Sometimes There
is almost an H in That
first syllable, and
sometimes a couple of
R's as well). But Kā-bool
no! Say The verses to
yourself and you'll find
They don't scan unless the
emphasis is on The first
syllable – as in This
song.

Ford, ford, ford o' Ka-bul riv-er.... Ford o' Ka-bul riv-er in the dark.... there's the
riv-er low an' fall-in', but it ain't no use a-call-in' 'cross the ford o' Ka-bul riv....er in....
the dark.

[23]

I feel sure that R.K, during his Lahore days, must have stopped in the course of a morning ride to watch a chain-gang being marched off by the police, and realising that one of them was a well-known dacoit, hailed him in the vernacular, and been so intrigued by his reply that he dismounted and walked beside him, talking to him.

It's the sort of thing he would have done; for like his little mongoose Rikki-Tikki-Tavi in The Jungle Book, he was eaten up from nose to tail with curiosity!

Not with an outcry to Allah nor any complaining
He answered his name at the muster and stood to the
      chaining.
When the twin anklets were nipped on the leg-bars that
      held them,
He brotherly greeted the armourers stooping to weld
      them.
Ere the sad dust of the marshalled feet of the chain-gang
      swallowed him,
Observing him nobly at ease, I alighted and followed him.
Thus we had speech by the way, but not touching his
      sorrow—
Rather his red Yesterday and his regal To-morrow,
Wherein he statelily moved to the clink of his chains
      unregarded,
Nowise abashed but contented to drink of the potion
      awarded.
Saluting aloofly his Fate, he made haste with his story,
And the words of his mouth were as slaves spreading
      carpets of glory
Embroidered with names of the Djinns—a miraculous
      weaving—
But the cool and perspicuous eye overbore unbelieving.
So I submitted myself to the limits of rapture—
Bound by this man we had bound, amid captives his
      capture—
Till he returned me to earth and the visions departed.
But on him be the Peace and the Blessing; for he was
      great-hearted!

[24]

Excerpt from

THE MASQUE OF PLENTY

INTERLUDE, *from Nowhere in Particular...*

Our cattle reel beneath the yoke they bear—
  The earth is iron and the skies are brass—
And faint with fervour of the flaming air
  The languid hours pass.

The well is dry beneath the village tree—
  The young wheat withers ere it reach a span,
And belts of blinding sand show cruelly
  Where once the river ran.

Pray, brothers, pray, but to no earthly King—
  Lift up your hands above the blighted grain,
Look westward—if they please, the Gods shall bring
  Their mercy with the rain.

Look westward—bears the blue no brown cloud-bank?
  Nay, it is written—wherefore should we fly?
On our own field and by our cattle's flank
  Lie down, lie down to die!

This is what happens
on the great plains
of Africa and Asia
when the rains fail.
Those who live
in western lands and
complain about
the climate do not
know how fortunate
they are.

[25]

'What are the bugles blowin' for?' said Files-on-Parade.
'To turn you out, to turn you out,' the Colour-Sergeant
      said.
'What makes you look so white, so white?' said Files-on-
      Parade.
'I'm dreadin' what I've got to watch,' the Colour-Sergeant
      said.
  For they're hangin' Danny Deever, you can hear the
      Dead March play,
  The Regiment's in 'ollow square—they're hangin' him
      to-day;
  They've taken of his buttons off an' cut his stripes
      away,
  An' they're hangin' Danny Deever in the mornin'.

'What makes the rear-rank breathe so 'ard?' said Files-on-
      Parade.
'It's bitter cold, it's bitter cold,' the Colour-Sergeant said.
'What makes that front-rank man fall down?' said Files-on-
      Parade.
'A touch o' sun, a touch o' sun,' the Colour-Sergeant said.
  They are hangin' Danny Deever, they are marchin' of
      'im round,
  They 'ave 'alted Danny Deever by 'is coffin on the
      ground;
  An' 'e'll swing in 'arf a minute for a sneakin' shootin'
      hound—
  O they're hangin' Danny Deever in the mornin'!

These extraordinary verses, the first of the famous 'Barrack-Room Ballads', appeared in the 'Scots Observer' less than two months after R.K's twenty-fourth birthday, and are said to have caused a learned authority on Milton, one Professor Masson, to electrify his students by brandishing a copy in class and shouting "Here's Literature! Here's Literature at last!"

'’Is cot was right-’and cot to mine,' said Files-on-Parade.
'’E's sleepin' out an' far to-night,' the Colour-Sergeant
  said.
'I've drunk 'is beer a score o' times,' said Files-on-Parade.
'’E's drinkin' bitter beer alone,' the Colour-Sergeant said.
  They are hangin' Danny Deever, you must mark 'im to
    'is place,
  For 'e shot a comrade sleepin'—you must look 'im in the
    face;
  Nine 'undred of 'is county an' the Regiment's disgrace,
  While they're hangin' Danny Deever in the mornin'.

'What's that so black agin the sun?' said Files-on-Parade.
'It's Danny fightin' 'ard for life,' the Colour-Sergeant said.
'What's that that whimpers over'ead?' said Files-on-
  Parade.
'It's Danny's soul that's passin' now,' the Colour-Sergeant
  said.
  For they're done with Danny Deever, you can 'ear the
    quickstep play,
  The Regiment's in column, an' they're marchin' us
    away;
  Ho! the young recruits are shakin', an' they'll want their
    beer to-day,
  After hangin' Danny Deever in the mornin'!

Like much of Kipling's verse, 'Danny Deever' was set to music, and I once heard that music played on its own by a Regimental Band. They began it with a bugle call and the music started quite softly and backed by the beat of the drums, got slower and heavier until, at the last, it suddenly switched to a brisk quickstep, with the pipes squealing – it sent cold shivers down my spine – even without the words.

[27]

The house named
Benmore was
the first club in Simla,
and the offices were
in a house not
far away called
Strawberry Hill. Then,
in some bureaucratic
re-shuffle, Strawberry
Hill became a private
house and Benmore –
a much larger house –
was turned into
offices.

Goff's maternal grand-
parents, General
Sir Godfrey and Lady
Adams-Williams,
lived at Strawberry Hill
for some years.
His mother was married
from there, and Goff
himself spent two
summers there as a
very small boy.

THE PLEA OF
THE SIMLA DANCERS

Too late, alas! the song
To remedy the wrong—
The rooms are taken from us, swept and garnished for their fate,
But these tear-besprinkled pages
Shall attest to future ages
That we cried against the crime of it—too late, alas! too late!

'What have *we* ever done to bear this grudge?'
    Was there no room save only in Benmore
For docket, *duftar*,[1] and for office-drudge,
    That you usurp our smoothest dancing floor?
Must Babus do their work on polished teak?
    Are ballrooms fittest for the ink you spill?
Was there no other cheaper house to seek?
    You might have left them all at Strawberry Hill.

We never harmed you! Innocent our guise,
    Dainty our shining feet, our voices low;
And we revolved to divers melodies,
    And we were happy but a year ago.
To-night, the moon that watched our lightsome wiles—
    That beamed upon us through the deodars—
Is wan with gazing on official files,
    And desecrating desks disgust the stars.

Nay! by the memory of tuneful nights—
    Nay! by the witchery of flying feet—
Nay! by the glamour of foredone delights—
    By all things merry, musical, and meet—
By wine that sparkled, and by sparkling eyes—
    By wailing waltz—by reckless galop's strain—
By dim verandahs and by soft replies.
    Give us our ravished ballroom back again!

[1] Office

[28]

Or—hearken to the curse we lay on you!
   The ghosts of waltzes shall perplex your brain,
And murmurs of past merriment pursue
   Your 'wildered clerks that they indite in vain;
And when you count your poor Provincial millions,
   The only figures that your pen shall frame
Shall be the figures of dear, dear cotillions
   Danced out in tumult long before you came.

Yea! '*See-Saw*' shall upset your estimates,
   '*Dream Faces*' shall your heavy heads bemuse.
Because your hand, unheeding, desecrates
   Our temple fit for higher, worthier use.
And all the long verandahs, eloquent
   With echoes of a score of Simla years,
Shall plague you with unbidden sentiment—
   Babbling of kisses, laughter, love, and tears.

So shall you mazed amid old memories stand,
   So shall you toil, and shall accomplish nought.
And ever in your ears a phantom Band
   Shall blare away the staid official thought.
Wherefore—and ere this awful curse be spoken,
   Cast out your swarthy sacrilegious train,
And give—ere dancing cease and hearts be broken—
   Give us our ravished ballroom back again!

[29]

Ay, lay him 'neath the Simla pine—
   A fortnight fully to be missed,
   Behold, we lose our fourth at whist,
A chair is vacant where we dine.

His place forgets him; other men
   Have bought his ponies, guns, and traps.
   His fortune is the Great Perhaps
And that cool rest-house down the glen,

Whence he shall hear, as spirits may,
   Our mundane revel on the height,
   Shall watch each flashing 'rickshaw-light
Sweep on to dinner, dance and play.

Benmore shall woo him to the ball
   With lighted rooms and braying band;
   And he shall hear and understand
'*Dream Faces*' better than us all.

For, think you, as the vapours flee
   Across Sanjaolie after rain,
   His soul may climb the hill again
To each old field of victory.

Unseen, whom women held so dear,
   The strong man's yearning to his kind
   Shall shake at most the window-blind,
Or dull awhile the card-room's cheer.

In his own place of power unknown,
   His Light o' Love another's flame,
   His dearest pony galloped lame,
And he an alien and alone!

Yet may he meet with many a friend—
　　Shrewd shadows, lingering long unseen
　　Among us when '*God save the Queen*'
Shows even 'extras' have an end.

And, when we leave the heated room,
　　And, when at four the lights expire,
　　The crew shall gather round the fire
And mock our laughter in the gloom;

Talk as we talked, and they ere death—
　　Flirt wanly, dance in ghostly wise,
　　With ghosts of tunes for melodies,
And vanish at the morning's breath!

'The Queen' in those days
was, of course, Victoria.
And in the ballroom
at Benmore (soon to
become an office block)
couples still waltzed the
nights away to
such romantic melodies
as 'Dream Faces'—and
attended far too many
funerals each season.
For this was the last
quarter of the 19th
century, and a time
when death was always
just around the
corner for the British
who served in India.
Death from typhoid,
tetanus, hydrophobia,
smallpox, cholera, sun-
stroke—you name it!

The price of Empire came
high.

THE LAST DEPARTMENT

Twelve hundred million men are spread
About this Earth, and I and You
Wonder, when You and I are dead,
'What will those luckless millions do?'

'None whole or clean,' we cry, 'or free from stain
Of favour.' Wait awhile, till we attain
   The Last Department where nor fraud nor fools,
Nor grade nor greed, shall trouble us again.

Fear, Favour, or Affection—what are these
To the grim Head who claims our services?
   I never knew a wife or interest yet
Delay that *pukka* step, miscalled 'decease';

When leave, long overdue, none can deny;
When idleness of all Eternity
   Becomes our furlough, and the marigold
Our thriftless, bullion-minting Treasury

Transferred to the Eternal Settlement,
Each in his strait, wood-scantled office pent,
   No longer Brown reverses Smith's appeals,
Or Jones records his Minute of Dissent.

And One, long since a pillar of the Court,
As mud between the beams thereof is wrought;
   And One who wrote on phosphates for the crops
Is subject-matter of his own Report.

These be the glorious ends whereto we pass—
Let Him who Is, go call on Him who Was;
   And He shall see the *mallie*[1] steals the slab
For curry-grinder, and for goats the grass.

[1] The cemetery gardener

[32]

The marigold is a funeral flower in Asia, and you can frequently see garlands of them, that have draped a corpse on its way to the burning ghat and been tossed with the ashes into the sacred waters of the Ganges, floating downstream on the current or lying stranded on a sandbank.

Nowadays I find they are used just as frequently in the garlands that are hung round the necks of arriving or departing friends, and as decoration at a wedding. I suppose because they are always in flower. But, when I was young marigolds meant funerals.

A breath of wind, a Border bullet's flight,
A draught of water, or a horse's fright—
   The droning of the fat *Sheristadar*[2]
Ceases, the punkah stops, and falls the night

For you or Me. Do those who live decline
The step that offers, or their work resign?
   Trust me, To-day's Most Indispensables,
Five hundred men can take your place or mine.

I remembered these verses when my father died very suddenly in Delhi, at the beginning of the hot-weather. We took his body up to the hills, to a little cemetary at Sanawar, among the foothills of the Himalayas, from where you can look out at one of the most beautiful views in the world.

From here, on a clear day, you can see the plains spread out before you like some ancient map on yellowed parchment that says 'Here be dragons', while below you lies the winding Simla road and the little cantonment town of Dugshai which was Tacklow's first station in India.

And to your left rise the true hills with behind them the long white line of the snows.

I had Tacklow's tombstone made from a curved block of sandstone wide enough to sit on comfortably, in the hope that other people – perhaps the boys from the Lawrence School at Sanawar? – would, if they ever visited the old cemetary (which by now must be disused) sit on it and look out at that fabulous view and realise what a beautiful country they have.

The inscription is on the inner side of the curve.

A BALLADE OF BURIAL
'Saint Praxed's ever was the Church for peace.'

If down here I chance to die,
  Solemnly I beg you take
All that is left of 'I'
  To the Hills for old sake's sake.
Pack me very thoroughly
  In the ice that used to slake
Pegs I drank when I was dry—
  This observe for old sake's sake.

To the railway station hie,
  There a single ticket take
For Umballa—goods-train—I
  Shall not mind delay or shake.
I shall rest contentedly
  Spite of clamour coolies make;
Thus in state and dignity
  Send me up for old sake's sake.

Next the sleepy Babu wake,
  Book a Kalka van 'for four'.
Few, I think, will care to make
  Journeys with me any more
As they used to do of yore.
  I shall need a 'special brake'—
'Thing I never took before—
  Get me one for old sake's sake.

After that—arrangements make.
  No hotel will take me in,
And a bullock's back would break
  'Neath the teak and leaden skin.
Tonga-ropes are frail and thin,
  Or, did I a back-seat take,
In a tonga I might spin,—
  Do your best for old sake's sake.

[34]

After that—your work is done.
    Recollect a Padre must
Mourn the dear departed one—
    Throw the ashes and the dust.
Don't go down at once. I trust
    You will find excuse to 'snake
Three days' casual on the bust,'[1]
    Get your fun for old sake's sake.

I could never stand the Plains.
    Think of blazing June and May,
Think of those September rains
    Yearly till the Judgment Day!
I should never rest in peacc,
    I should sweat and lie awake.
Rail me then, on my decease,
    To the Hills for old sake's sake!

A lot of death in These last few pages, I notice; and in other verses in This book, too. But there was a lot of death in India in Kipling's day.

[1] Three days' leave

[35]

PAGETT, MP

The toad beneath the harrow knows
Exactly where each tooth-point goes;
The butterfly upon the road
Preaches contentment to that toad.

Pagett, MP, was a liar, and a fluent liar therewith,—
He spoke of the heat of India as 'The Asian Solar Myth';
'Came on a four months' visit, to 'study the East' in November,
And I got him to make an agreement vowing to stay till
     September.

March came in with the *koïl*.[1] Pagett was cool and gay,
Called me a 'bloated Brahmin,' talked of my 'princely pay.'
March went out with the roses. 'Where is your heat?' said he.
'Coming,' said I to Pagett. 'Skittles!' said Pagett, MP.

April began with the punkah, coolies, and prickly-heat,—
Pagett was dear to mosquitoes, sandflies found him a treat.
He grew speckled and lumpy—hammered, I grieve to say,
Aryan brothers who fanned him, in an illiberal way.

May set in with a dust-storm,—Pagett went down with the sun.
All the delights of the season tickled him one by one.
Imprimis—ten days' 'liver'—due to his drinking beer;
Later, a dose of fever—slight, but he called it severe.

Dysent'ry touched him in June, after the *Chota Bursat*[2]—
Lowered his portly person—made him yearn to depart.
He didn't call me a 'Brahmin,' or 'bloated,' or 'over-paid,'
But seemed to think it a wonder that any one ever stayed.

July was a trifle unhealthy,—Pagett was ill with fear,
Called it the 'Cholera Morbus,' hinted that life was dear.
He babbled of 'Eastern exile,' and mentioned his home with tears;
But I hadn't seen *my* children for close upon seven years.

[1] The Indian bell-bird   [2] The early rains

[36]

We reached a hundred and twenty once in the Court at noon,
(I've mentioned Pagett was portly) Pagett went off in a swoon.
That was an end to the business. Pagett, the perjured, fled
With a practical, working knowledge of 'Solar Myths' in his head.

And I laughed as I drove from the station, but the mirth died
    out on my lips
As I thought of the fools like Pagett who write of their
    'Eastern trips;'
And the sneers of the travelled idiots who duly misgovern
    the land,
And I prayed to the Lord to deliver another one into my hand.

Kipling must have met a Paget M.P.
India was stiff with Them during the cold
weather, but they were strictly migrants, and
left before the heat and the mosquitoes
got going. They also always knew better
than you, and invariably produced the
same reason why this should be so:
"The onlooker sees most of the game!"
Well yes, But he doesn't get any of the hard
knocks, broken bones, bruises, sprains
and black eyes!
These were the verses that Kipling signed
'An Englishman', and that were cut out of
the Civil and Military Gazette by my
Aunt Molly and pasted in her
photograph-cum-scrap album, which
now belongs to her grandson, my cousin
Peter Hamblyn.

[37]

In mediæval days a candidate
for knighthood had to go
through a series of ceremonies
That began with a bath
and included a night-long
vigil on his knees
before the altar of an empty
church, followed by
various rituals such as the
laying on of the sword,
the buckling of The swordbelt
and spurs, and so on.
Nowadays he kneels briefly
before his monarch who
taps him on both shoulders
with a small dress sword and
says: "Arise, Sir so and so"
And That's it!

This is only that old nursery
rhyme 'Who killed Cock Robin?'
with variations.
But as a character in one of
R.K's stories says (and it
could have been R.K speaking
"Yes—but I did the variations!")

THE NEW KNIGHTHOOD

Who gives him the Bath?
'I,' said the wet,
 Rank Jungle-sweat,
'I'll give him the Bath!'

Who'll sing the psalms?
'We,' said the Palms.
'As the hot wind becalms,
'We'll sing the psalms.'

Who lays on the sword?
'I,' said the Sun,
'Before he has done,
'I'll lay on the sword.'

Who fastens his belt?
'I,' said Short-Rations,
'I know all the fashions
'Of tightening a belt!'

Who gives him his spur?
'I,' said his Chief,
 Exacting and brief,
'I'll give him the spur.'

Who'll shake his hand?
'I,' said the Fever,
'And I'm no deceiver,
'I'll shake his hand.'

Who brings him the wine?
'I,' said Quinine,
'It's a habit of mine.
'I'll come with his wine.'

[38]

Who'll put him to proof?
'I,' said All Earth.
'Whatever he's worth,
'I'll put to the proof.'

Who'll choose him for Knight?
'I,' said his Mother,
'Before any other,
'My very own Knight.'

And after this fashion, adventure to seek,
Was Sir Galahad made—as it might be last week!

'GIFFEN'S DEBT' SHARP

Once again I am
fascinated by the ease
with which Kipling
handles any type of
verse.
He did not often write
blank verse. But as
with his 'Sestina of
The Tramp Royal',
when he does, one
hardly notices what he
is up to because
it flows so smoothly.

A 'griffen', by the way
was, at that date, a
slang-word for a
newly-joined subaltern
fresh out from home.
I don't know whether
that was why
Kipling called the
ne'er-do-well in these
verses 'Giffen'.
Possibly?

This is yet another
tale that is based on a
true story that R.K
probably picked up in
his wanderings
around India as a
cub-reporter. The
same way he picked

Imprimis he was 'broke'. Thereafter left
His Regiment and, later, took to drink;
Then, having lost the balance of his friends,
'Went Fantee'—joined the people of the land,
Turned three parts Mussulman and one Hindu,
And lived among the Gauri villagers,
Who gave him shelter and a wife or twain,
And boasted that a thorough, full-blood *sahib*
Had come among them. Thus he spent his time,
Deeply indebted to the village *shroff* [1]
(Who never asked for payment), always drunk,
Unclean, abominable, out-at-heels;
Forgetting that he was an Englishman.

You know they dammed the Gauri with a dam,
And all the good contractors scamped their work
And all the bad material at hand
Was used to dam the Gauri—which was cheap,
And, therefore, proper. Then the Gauri burst,
And several hundred thousand cubic tons
Of water dropped into the valley, *flop*,
And drowned some five-and-twenty villagers,
And did a lakh or two of detriment
To crops and cattle. When the flood went down
We found him dead, beneath an old dead horse
Full six miles down the valley. So we said
He was a victim of the Demon Drink,
And moralised upon him for a week,
And then forgot him. Which was natural.

But, in the valley of the Gauri, men
Beneath the shadow of the big new dam,
Relate a foolish legend of the flood,
Accounting for the little loss of life
(Only those five-and-twenty villagers)
In this wise:—On the evening of the flood,

[42]

They heard the groaning of the rotten dam,
And voices of the Mountain Devils. Then
An incarnation of the local God,
Mounted upon a monster-neighing horse,
And flourishing a flail-like whip, came down,
Breathing ambrosia, to the villages,
And fell upon the simple villagers
With yells beyond the power of mortal throat,
And blows beyond the power of mortal hand,
And smote them with his flail-like whip, and drove
Them clamorous with terror up the hill,
And scattered, with the monster-neighing steed,
Their crazy cottages about their ears,
And generally cleared those villages.
Then came the water, and the local God,
Breathing ambrosia, flourishing his whip,
And mounted on his monster-neighing steed,
Went down the valley with the flying trees
And residue of homesteads, while they watched
Safe on the mountain-side these wondrous things,
And knew that they were much beloved of Heaven.

Wherefore, and when the dam was newly built,
They raised a temple to the local God,
And burnt all manner of unsavoury things
Upon his altar, and created priests,
And blew into a conch and banged a bell,
And told the story of the Gauri flood
With circumstance and much embroidery . . .
So he, the whiskified Objectionable,
Unclean, abominable, out-at-heels,
Became the Tutelary Deity
Of all the Gauri valley villages,
And may in time become a Solar Myth.

up the material for a short story that he called 'The Tomb of his Ancestors'. There was a tomb in that too. The tomb of an Englishman that had become a shrine.

There are any number of tombs scattered around India, some dating from as far back as the 17th Century, which mark the spot where the bones of some long-dead white man in the service of the East India Company lie: his name forgotten but his memory kept green by the descendents of villagers or townsfolk whom he once helped or was good to, and who bring offerings and light lamps made from cotton wicks floating in earthenware saucers filled with oil, in remembrance of past-kindness. Asia has a long memory.

The inscription on the tomb of 'Parry's Mound' in a novel I wrote called 'Shadow of the Moon', was taken from a real tombstone stumbled on by chance by a shooting party in what was then the United Provinces. I only altered the surname, nothing else. The date was 1666.

This is the young Kipling feeling homesick for England, and, I suppose, these verses must have spoken for all Anglo-Indians who felt themselves to be exiles and dreamed of Home and the day they would be able to retire and settle down in their native land for keeps. I knew a good number of this type myself, and could sympathise with them. Though having been born in India, I could not share their feelings.

To them Christmas was snow and grey skies, carols and holly, and candles on a christmas tree. But to me it was the country-side that Kipling has described in these verses, plus the glamour and excitement of going into camp on the plains, or by one of the great rivers of the Punjab.

Dim dawn behind the tamarisks—the sky is saffron-yellow—
  As the women in the village grind the corn,
And the parrots seek the river-side, each calling to his fellow
  That the Day, the staring Eastern Day, is born.
    O the white dust on the highway! O the stenches in
      the byway!
      O the clammy fog that hovers over earth!
    And at Home they're making merry 'neath the white
      and scarlet berry—
      What part have India's exiles in their mirth?

Full day behind the tamarisks—the sky is blue and staring—
  As the cattle crawl afield beneath the yoke,
And they bear One o'er the field-path, who is past all hope
      or caring,
  To the ghat below the curling wreaths of smoke.
    Call on Rama, going slowly, as ye bear a brother lowly—
      Call on Rama—he may hear, perhaps, your voice!
    With our hymn-books and our psalters we appeal to
      other altars,
      And to-day we bid 'good Christian men rejoice!'

High noon behind the tamarisks—the sun is hot above us—
  As at Home the Christmas Day is breaking wan.
They will drink our healths at dinner—those who tell us how
      they love us,
  And forget us till another year be gone!
    O the toil that knows no breaking! O the *Heimweh*,
      ceaseless, aching!
      O the black dividing Sea and alien Plain!
    Youth was cheap—wherefore we sold it. Gold was good—
      we hoped to hold it.
      And to-day we know the fulness of our gain!

[44]

Grey dusk behind the tamarisks—the parrots fly together—
    As the Sun is sinking slowly over Home;
And his last ray seems to mock us shackled in a lifelong tether
    That drags us back howe'er so far we roam.
      Hard her service, poor her payment—she in ancient,
        tattered raiment—
        India, she the grim Stepmother of our kind.
      If a year of life be lent her, if her temple's shrine we
        enter,
        The door is shut—we may not look behind.

Black night behind the tamarisks—the owls begin their chorus—
    As the conches from the temple scream and bray.
With the fruitless years behind us and the hopeless years
        before us,
    Let us honour, O my brothers, Christmas Day!
      Call a truce, then, to our labours—let us feast with
        friends and neighbours,
        And be merry as the custom of our caste;
      For, if 'faint and forced the laughter,' and if sadness
        follow after,
        We are richer by one mocking Christmas past.

India may have been a 'grim stepmother' to many of The British who served her. And to most of them her service was indeed hard and poorly-paid. But we who had the good fortune to be born in her land and feel at home in it, loved her dearly. Never more so than under canvas at Christmas time.

[45]

Here is R.K feeling homesick again! – This time as the weather begins to hot up in Lahore.

Interesting to compare these verses with his 'Song of the wise children', in which, as a middle-aged Pater-familias, he writes of delight he feels in escaping from the icy winds of an English winter to the hot blue skies, the blazing sun and the palm trees of his youth.

The little koïl is an Indian bell-bird, and its maddening song is one of the horrors of a hot-weather in the plains. It used to be known as the 'brain-fever bird' for its call, which starts at the bottom of a short scale and finishes on a high note, and is repeated over and over again, and sounds exactly like "Brain-fever! Brain-fever! Brain-fever!"

The Sāt-bhai, which means seven brothers, aquired that name because they tend to go around in groups of seven – count 'em and see! Personally, I've always thought of them as groups of gossiping spinsters. And others must have had the same idea, for the British always called those birds 'seven sisters'. Never seven brothers.

My garden blazes brightly with the rose-bush and the
  peach,
  And the *koïl* sings above it, in the *siris* by the well,
From the creeper-covered trellis comes the squirrel's
  chattering speech,
  And the blue jay screams and flutters where the
  cheery *sat-bhai* dwell.
But the rose has lost its fragrance, and the *koïl*'s
  note is strange;
  I am sick of endless sunshine, sick of blossom-
  burdened bough.
Give me back the leafless woodlands where the
  winds of Springtime range—
  Give me back one day in England, for it's Spring in
  England now!

Through the pines the gusts are booming, o'er the
  brown fields blowing chill,
  From the furrow of the ploughshare streams the
  fragrance of the loam,
And the hawk nests on the cliffside and the jackdaw
  in the hill,
  And my heart is back in England 'mid the sights and
  sounds of Home.
But the garland of the sacrifice this wealth of rose and
  peach is
  Ah! *koïl*, little *koïl*, singing on the *siris* bough,
In my ears the knell of exile your ceaseless bell like
  speech is—
  Can *you* tell me aught of England or of Spring in
  England now?

[46]

THE LOVE SONG
OF HAR DYAL

Alone upon the housetops to the North
I turn and watch the lightnings in the sky—
The glamour of thy footsteps in the North.
Come back to me, Beloved, or I die.

Below my feet the still bazar is laid—
Far, far below the weary camels lie—
The camels and the captives of thy raid.
Come back to me, Beloved, or I die!

My father's wife is old and harsh with years,
And drudge of all my father's house am I—
My bread is sorrow and my drink is tears.
Come back to me, Beloved, or I die!

These three short verses were once the means of turning a friend of mine from a Kipling-hater to a life-long fan. He had given me a lift home after a dinner-party at a house some miles from Peshawar, which is on the North West Frontier of what was then British India and is now Pakistan.

There was a bright moon, and despite the lateness of the hour the night was breathlessly hot, for it was early June. The streets and bazaars on the outskirts of the city were silent and deserted, and nothing moved except my friend's ancient Ford and the summer lightening that flickered in the sky beyond the barren Kyber Hills.

Only one person besides ourselves appeared to be awake; a lone woman standing on the flat roof-top of one of the houses and looking towards the hills.
"Har Dyal, I presume", I said without thinking.
"Har who?" enquired my friend.
I recited these verses and he said: "Nice. Who wrote it?"
"Kipling".
"Kipling? You mean that fellow who wrote those awful cockney jingo-jingles?"
I replied suitably. And believe it or not, it turned out that he had never read anything at all by Kipling. Not even one single 'awful cockney jingo-jingle'! Not even Danny Deever! His comment was merely based on hearsay and prejudice. However I am happy to relate that next day he borrowed my 'Rudyard Kipling's Inclusive Verse' and never looked back.

R.K repeated this opinion in 'Puck of Pooks Hill'— "Write to any man that all is betrayed", said De Aquila "and even the Pope himself would sleep uneasily, Eh, Jehan? If one told thee all was betrayed what wouldst thou do?" "I would run away" said Jehan. "It might be true".

Cry 'Murder' in the market-place, and each
Will turn upon his neighbour anxious eyes
Asking: 'Art thou the man?' We hunted Cain
Some centuries ago across the world.
This bred the fear our own misdeeds maintain
To-day.

His Wedded Wife

They burnt a corpse upon the sand—
The light shone out afar;
It guided home the plunging dhows
That beat from Zanzibar.
Spirit of Fire, where'er Thy altars rise,
Thou art the Light of Guidance to our eyes!

In Error

How many people down the long centuries must have thought this and would have given anything in return for that 'one moments comfort'? Kipling was probably not twenty when he wrote this —possibly less. Yet few people could have put it better. And in the event he was to be one of the lucky ones because I have heard it said that he bought his Sussex house, Batemans, because he saw, or thought he saw, the ghost of seven-year-old Josephine, his adored and adorable little daughter whose death had cracked his heart, looking out of one of the upstairs windows.

Not though you die to-night, O Sweet, and wail,
A spectre at my door,
Shall mortal Fear make Love immortal fail—
I shall but love you more,
Who, from Death's House returning, give me still
One moment's comfort in my matchless ill.

By Word of Mouth

Pit where the buffalo cooled his hide,
By the hot sun emptied, and blistered and dried;
Log in the plume-grass, hidden and lone;
Bund where the earth-rat's mounds are strown;
Cave in the bank where the sly stream steals;
Aloe that stabs at the belly and heels,
Jump if you dare on a steed untried—
Safer it is to go wide—go wide!
Hark, from in front where the best men ride;—
'Pull to the off, boys! Wide! Go wide!'

Cupid's Arrows

We be the Gods of the East—
    Older than all—
Masters of Mourning and Feast—
    How shall we fall?

Will they gape for the husks that ye proffer
    Or yearn to your song?
And we—have we nothing to offer
    Who ruled them so long—
In the fume of the incense, the clash of the cymbals,
    the blare of the conch and the gong?

Over the strife of the schools
    Low the day burns—
Back with the kine from the pools
    Each one returns
To the life that he knows where the altar-flame glows
    and the *tulsi*[1] is trimmed in the urns.

The Naulahka

[1]The Holy Basil

[49]

The Naulahka is the title of an undistinguished novel that Kipling wrote in collaboration with a spell-binding young American, Wolcott Balastier, with whom he had become so besotted that when Wolcott died very suddenly of typhoid, and more or less left his sister Carrie to Rudyard as a death-bed bequest. The grief-stricken beneficiary (who happened to be on the other side of the world at the time) rushed back to London to marry his legacy by special license in icy weather and in the presence of only five wedding guests. The rest were all down with 'flu.

It would be interesting to know what sort of person he would have been if he had married someone peaceful and charming instead of a jealous, possessive and bossy jumping bean who turned the once brash and extrovert Ruddy into the guarded and suspicious celebrity so often referred to by journalists and biographers as "This intensely private man".
He certainly wasn't 'intensely private' before Carrie went to work on him!

'Beast and Man in India' was a book written and illustrated by Rudyard's father John Lockwood Kipling. His son wrote the chapter headings for him. These are two of them.

In many eastern countries a goat is still sacrificed to avert ill-fortune or to bring good-luck.

When Goff and I were in Pakistan in 1979, we were taken by helicopter into Tribal Territory to visit the scene of a long-ago battle in which the Guides had suffered heavy casualties, and Goff had been wounded. There was an old Picket on a ridge overlooking the battlefield (a picket is a small defended outpost that would be manned by two or three men). When he told his hosts that it was one that he had helped to build all those years ago, they told him that in future it would be known as 'Hamilton's Picket', and that a goat would duly be sacrificed to confirm it.
Such a sacrifice is never wasted, for the flesh is roasted and provides a banquet, and there are endless uses for the skin.

They killed a Child to please the Gods
In Earth's young penitence,
And I have bled in that Babe's stead
Because of innocence.

I bear the sins of sinful men
That have no sin of my own,
They drive me forth to Heaven's wrath
Unpastured and alone.

I am the meat of sacrifice,
The ransom of man's guilt,
For they give my life to the altar-knife
Wherever shrine is built.

The Goat

The beasts are very wise,
Their mouths are clean of lies,
They talk one to the other,
Bullock to bullock's brother
Resting after their labours,
Each in stall with his neighbours.
But man with goad and whip
Breaks up their fellowship,
Shouts in their silky ears
Filling their soul with fears.
When he has ploughed the land,
He says: 'They understand.'
But the beasts in stall together,
Freed from the yoke and tether,
Say as the torn flanks smoke:
'Nay, 'twas the whip that spoke.'

[50]

I will remember what I was. I am sick of rope and chain—
    I will remember my old strength and all my forest-affairs.
I will not sell my back to man for a bundle of sugar-cane.
    I will go out to my own kind, and the wood-folk in their lairs.

I will go out until the day, until the morning break,
    Out to the winds' untainted kiss, the waters' clean caress.
I will forget my ankle-ring and snap my picket-stake.
    I will revisit my lost loves, and playmates masterless!

Toomai of the Elephants

Kipling had a habit of writing verses to accompany all his short stories, and these were written for one of my favourite 'Jungle Book' tales, 'Toomai of the Elephants'. Anyone who hasn't read it should do so at once; and here is just a small taste of it; Toomai, asleep in the Elephant lines has woken in bright moonlight to see his father's elephant, Kala Nag, standing up with his ears cocked:

"Little Toomai turned, rustling in the fodder, and watched the curve of his big back against half the stars of heaven; and while he watched he heard, so far away that it sounded no more than a pinhole of noise pricked through the stillness, the 'hoot-toot of a wild elephant'"

[51]

The Song of
The Little Hunter

Ere Mor the Peacock flutters, ere the Monkey People cry,
  Ere Chil the Kite swoops down a furlong sheer,
Through the Jungle very softly flits a shadow and a sigh—
  He is Fear, O Little Hunter, he is Fear!
Very softly down the glade runs a waiting, watching shade,
  And the whisper spreads and widens far and near.
And the sweat is on thy brow, for he passes even now—
  He is Fear, O Little Hunter, he is Fear!

Ere the moon has climbed the mountain, ere the rocks are
        ribbed with light,
  When the downward-dipping trails are dank and drear,
Comes a breathing hard behind thee—*snuffle-snuffle* through
        the night—
  It is Fear, O Little Hunter, it is Fear!
On thy knees and draw the bow; bid the shrilling arrow go;
  In the empty, mocking thicket plunge the spear!
But thy hands are loosed and weak, and the blood has left
        thy cheek—
  It is Fear, O Little Hunter, it is Fear!

When the heat-cloud sucks the tempest, when the slivered
        pine-trees fall,
  When the blinding, blaring rain-squalls lash and veer,
Through the war-gongs of the thunder rings a voice more
        loud than all—
  It is Fear, O Little Hunter, it is Fear!
Now the spates are banked and deep; now the footless
        boulders leap—
  Now the lightning shows each littlest leaf-rib clear—
But thy throat is shut and dried, and thy heart against thy side
  Hammers: Fear, O Little Hunter—this is Fear!

[52]

MORNING SONG
IN THE JUNGLE

One moment past our bodies cast
    No shadow on the plain;
Now clear and black they stride our track,
    And we run home again.
In morning-hush, each rock and bush
    Stands hard, and high, and raw:
Then give the Call: *'Good rest to all*
    That keep the Jungle Law!'

Now horn and pelt our peoples melt
    In covert to abide;
Now, crouched and still, to cave and hill
    Our Jungle Barons glide.
Now, stark and plain, Man's oxen strain,
    That draw the new-yoked plough;
Now, stripped and dread, the dawn is red
    Above the lit *talao*[1].

Ho! Get to lair! The sun's aflare
    Behind the breathing grass:
And creaking through the young bamboo
    The warning whispers pass.
By day made strange, the woods we range
    With blinking eyes we scan;
While down the skies the wild duck cries:
    'The Day—the Day to Man!'

The dew is dried that drenched our hide,
    Or washed about our way;
And where we drank, the puddled bank
    Is crisping into clay.
The traitor Dark gives up each mark
    Of stretched or hooded claw:
Then hear the Call: *'Good rest to all*
    That keep the Jungle Law!'

[1]pond or lake

[53]

'Blessèd be the English and all their ways and works.
 Cursèd be the Infidels, Hereticks, and Turks!'
'Amen,' quo' Jobson, 'but where I used to lie
 Was neither Candle, Bell nor Book to curse my brethren by,

'But a palm-tree in full bearing, bowing down, bowing down,
 To a surf that drove unsparing at the brown, walled town—
 Conches in a temple, oil-lamps in a dome—
 And a low moon out of Africa said: "This way home!"'

'Blessèd be the English and all that they profess.
 Cursèd be the Savages that prance in nakedness!'
'Amen,' quo' Jobson, 'but where I used to lie
 Was neither shirt nor pantaloons to catch my brethren by:

'But a well-wheel slowly creaking, going round, going round,
 By a water-channel leaking over drowned, warm ground—
 Parrots very busy in the trellised pepper-vine—
 And a high sun over Asia shouting: "Rise and shine!"'

'Blessèd be the English and everything they own.
 Cursèd be the Infidels that bow to wood and stone!'
'Amen,' quo' Jobson, 'but where I used to lie
 Was neither pew nor Gospelleer to save my brethren by:

'But a desert stretched and stricken, left and right, left and right,
 Where the piled mirages thicken under white-hot light—
 A skull beneath a sand-hill and a viper coiled inside—
 And a red wind out of Libya roaring: "Run and hide!"'

'Blessèd be the English and all they make or do.
 Cursèd be the Hereticks who doubt that this is true!'
'Amen,' quo' Jobson, 'but where I mean to die
 Is neither rule nor calliper to judge the matter by:

[54]

'But Himalaya heavenward-heading, sheer and vast, sheer and vast,
In a million summits bedding on the last world's past—
A certain sacred mountain where the scented cedars climb,
And—the feet of my Belovèd hurrying back through Time!'

This poem says everything that I
feel about the East. 'Amen' to it all,
Dear Jobson!

[55]

'MANDALAY'

Part Two

THE EXILES' LINE

Kipling has written This
as a skit on The
Rubáiyát of Omar
Khayyám, and must
have had a lot of fun
in The process.
Edward Fitzgeralds'
translation of The
Rubáiyat was fairly
new in Those days,
and The schoolboy
Ruddy had been
charmed by it.

Someone jumped or
fell overboard on The
first night of my very
first voyage on a
liner.
See verse five!

Now the New Year reviving old desires,
The restless soul to open sea aspires,
    Where the Blue Peter flickers from the fore,
And the grimed stoker feeds the engine-fires.

Coupons, alas, depart with all their rows,
And last year's sea-met loves where Grindlay knows;
    But still the wild wind wakes off Gardafui,
And hearts turn eastward with the P&O's.

Twelve knots an hour, be they more or less—
Oh, slothful mother of much idleness,
    Whom neither rivals spur nor contracts speed!
Nay, bear us gently! Wherefore need we press?

The Tragedy of all our East is laid
On those white decks beneath the awning shade—
    Birth, absence, longing, laughter, love and tears,
And death unmaking ere the land is made.

And midnight madnesses of souls distraught
Whom the cool seas call through the open port,
    So that the table lacks one place next morn,
And for one forenoon men forgo their sport.

The shadow of the rigging to and fro
Sways, shifts, and flickers on the spar-deck's snow,
    And like a giant trampling in his chains,
The screw-blades gasp and thunder deep below;

And, leagued to watch one flying-fish's wings,
Heaven stoops to sea, and sea to Heaven clings;
    While, bent upon the ending of his toil,
The hot sun strides, regarding not these things:

[58]

For the same wave that meets our stem in spray
Bore Smith of Asia eastward yesterday,
　　And Delhi Jones and Brown of Midnapore
To-morrow follow on the self-same way.

Linked in the chain of Empire one by one,
Flushed with long leave, or tanned with many a sun,
　　The Exiles' Line brings out the exiles' line,
And ships them homeward when their work is done.

Yea, heedless of the shuttle through the loom,
The flying keels fulfil the web of doom.
　　Sorrow or shouting—what is that to them?
Make out the cheque that pays for cabin-room!

And how so many score of times ye flit
With wife and babe and caravan of kit,
　　Not all thy travels past shall lower one fare,
Not all thy tears abate one pound of it.

And how so high thine earth-born dignity,
Honour and state, go sink it in the sea,
　　Till that great one upon the quarter-deck,
Brow-bound with gold, shall give thee leave to be.

Indeed, indeed from that same line we swear
Off for all time, and mean it when we swear;
　　And then, and then we meet the Quartered Flag,
And, surely for the last time, pay the fare.

And Green of Kensington, estrayed to view
In three short months the world he never knew,
　　Stares with blind eyes upon the Quartered Flag
And sees no more than yellow, red and blue.

But we, the gipsies of the east, but we—
Waifs of the land and wastrels of the sea—
　　Come nearer home beneath the Quartered Flag
Than ever home shall come to such as we.

[59]

One of the nicest things about those voyages was watching the shoals of flying-fishes take off from the top of a wave and skitter away across the dark, sapphire blue of the Indian Ocean like handfuls of jewels.

I could watch them for hours.

The camp is struck, the bungalow decays,
Dead friends and houses desert mark our ways,
 Till sickness send us down to Prince's Dock
To meet the changeless use of many days.

Bound in the wheel of Empire, one by one,
The chain-gangs of the East from sire to son,
 The Exiles' Line takes out the exiles' line
And ships them homeward when their work is done.

How runs the old indictment? 'Dear and slow,'
So much and twice so much. We gird, but go.
 For all the soul of our sad East is there,
Beneath the house-flag of the P&O.

Kipling once wrote that 'certain families serve India generation after generation as dolphins follow in a line across the open sea'. And most of those men and their families were transported Eastward to their labours in a steamship of the Peninsular and Orient Line: the famous P&O. For over a century it took us out and brought us home again, and we knew and loved it.

I myself, who like so many of us, was born in that country, was three years old when I took the first of many voyages on the Exiles Line,— though for me the exile was from India not England.

The P&O was responsible for the slang word 'posh', meaning smart or grand. It came from the initials 'Port-side Out, Starboard Home' because the richer or more senior passengers reserved the cabins on the shady side of the ship — which was the port side going East and the starboard side going West.

Dear P&O. How I loved those voyages. "No more, no more the folly and the fun! Our little day was brave and gay — but now it's done."

THE RECALL

I am the land of their fathers.
In me the virtue stays.
I will bring back my children,
After certain days.

Under their feet in the grasses
My clinging magic runs.
They shall return as strangers.
They shall remain as sons.

Over their heads in the branches
Of their new-bought, ancient trees,
I weave an incantation
And draw them to my knees.

Scent of smoke in the evening,
Smell of rain in the night—
The hours, the days and the seasons,
Order their souls aright,

Till I make plain the meaning
Of all my thousand years—
Till I fill their hearts with knowledge,
While I fill their eyes with tears.

I know that Kipling must have been thinking of his own country when he wrote this. Probably of his chosen county, Sussex. But to me it will always mean the land of my birth, my childhood and my youth, whose 'clinging magic' still continues to draw me back. It works both ways; for an Indian friend of mine, who had been to school and then college in England and wanted to stay there, told me that his father said he must of course do exactly what he wished; but that one day he would come back to India: and quoted this poem to him to prove it!

[61]

A well-known patron of
The Victorian Music-halls,
Richard Le Gallienne,
editor of The Liberal
Star, who was a great
admirer of The 'Barrack-
Room Ballads', considered
This one to be The best
of Them; even Though
it was "made out of the
very refuse of language(!)

It was, of course, put to
music, and one still
hears it occasionally
on The radio, or sung on
T.V. by some concert
baritone – in These days
always to the wrong
tune.
The original one was
better. Or do I only
Think so because That
earlier tune sticks in
my head, and That is
the way I hear The
song?
Charles Carrington
who Kipling's daughter
chose to write her
father's biography, says
That Kipling wrote
'Mandalay' to The
tune of a popular
waltz – but he doesn't
say what waltz!

By the old Moulmein Pagoda, lookin' lazy at the sea,
There's a Burma girl a-settin', and I know she thinks o' me;
For the wind is in the palm-trees, and the temple-bells
    they say:
'Come you back, you British soldier; come you back to
    Mandalay!'
      Come you back to Mandalay,
      Where the old Flotilla lay:
      Can't you 'ear their paddles chunkin' from
        Rangoon to Mandalay?
      On the road to Mandalay,
      Where the flyin'-fishes play,
      An' the dawn comes up like thunder outer
        China 'crost the Bay!

'Er petticoat was yaller an' 'er little cap was green,
An' 'er name was Supi-yaw-lat—jes' the same as Theebaw's
    Queen,
An' I seed her first a-smokin' of a whackin' white cheroot,
An' a-wastin' Christian kisses on an 'eathen idol's foot:
      Bloomin' idol made o' mud—
      Wot they called the Great Gawd Budd—
      Plucky lot she cared for idols when I kissed 'er
        where she stud!
      On the road to Mandalay . . .

When the mist was on the rice-fields an' the sun was
    droppin' slow,
She'd git 'er little banjo an' she'd sing 'Kulla-lo-lo!'
With 'er arm upon my shoulder an' 'er cheek agin my cheek
We useter watch the steamers an' the *hathis* pilin' teak.
      Elephints a-pilin' teak
      In the sludgy, squdgy creek,
      Where the silence 'ung that 'eavy you was 'arf
        afraid to speak!
      On the road to Mandalay . . .

[62]

But that's all shove be'ind me—long ago an' fur away,
An' there ain't no 'buses runnin' from the Bank to Mandalay;
An' I'm learnin' 'ere in London what the ten-year soldier tells:
'If you've 'eard the East a-callin', you won't never 'eed
      naught else.'
        No! you won't 'eed nothin' else
        But them spicy garlic smells,
        An' the sunshine an' the palm-trees an' the
          tinkly temple-bells;
        On the road to Mandalay . . .

I am sick o' wastin' leather on these gritty pavin'-stones,
An' the blasted English drizzle wakes the fever in my bones;
Tho' I walks with fifty 'ousemaids outer Chelsea to the
      Strand,
An' they talks a lot o' lovin', but wot do they understand?
        Beefy face an' grubby 'and—
        Law! wot do they understand?
        I've a neater, sweeter maiden in a cleaner,
          greener land!
        On the road to Mandalay . . .

Ship me somewheres east of Suez, where the best is like
      the worst,
Where there aren't no Ten Commandments an' a man can
      raise a thirst;
For the temple-bells are callin', an' it's there that I would be—
By the old Moulmein Pagoda, looking lazy at the sea;
        On the road to Mandalay,
        Where the old Flotilla lay,
        With our sick beneath the awnings when we
          went to Mandalay!
        O the road to Mandalay,
        Where the flyin'-fishes play,
        An' the dawn comes up like thunder outer
          China 'crost the Bay!

A SONG IN THE DESERT

Friend, thou beholdest the lightning? Who has the charge of it—
To decree which rock-ridge shall receive—shall be chosen for
      targe of it?
Which crown among palms shall go down, by the thunderbolt
      broken;
While the floods drown the sere wadis where no bud is token?

First for my eyes, above all, he made show of his treasure.
First in his ear, before all, I made sure of my measure.
If it were good—what acclaim! None other so moved me.
If it were faulty—what shame? While he mocked me he loved me.

Friend, thou hast seen in Rida'ar, the low moon descending,
One silent, swart, swift-striding camel, oceanward wending?
Browbound and jawbound the rider, his shadow in front of him,
Ceaselessly eating the distances? That was the wont of him.

Whether the cliff-walled defiles, the ambush prepared for him;
Whether the wave-crested dunes—a single sword bared for him—
Whether cold danger fore-weighed, or quick peril that took him
Alone, out of comfort or aid, no breath of it shook him.

Whether he feasted or fasted, sweated or shivered,
There was no proof of the matter—no sign was delivered.
Whatever this dust or that heat, or those fools that he laboured
      with,
He forgot and forbore no observance towards any he neighboured
      with.

Friend, thou has known at Rida'ar, when the Council was bidden,
One face among faces that leaped to the light and were hidden?
One voice among night-wasting voices of boasting and shouting?
And that face and that voice abide with thee? His beyond doubting!

Never again in Rida'ar, my watch-fire burning,
That he might see from afar, shall I wait his returning;
Or the roar of his beast as she knelt and he leaped to unlade her,
Two-handedly tossing me jewels. *He* was no trader!

Gems and wrought gold, never sold—brought for me to behold
     them;
Tales of far magic unrolled—to me only he told them,
With the light, easy laugh of dismissal 'twixt story and story—
As a man brushes sand from his hand, or the great dismiss glory.

Never again in Rida'ar! My ways are made black to me!
Whether I sing or am silent, he shall not come back to me!
There is no measure for trial, nor treasure for bringing.
Allah divides the Companions. (*Yet he said—yet he said:*—
     'Cease not from singing.')

Kipling wrote these verses in memory of a famous
War Correspondent, Percival Landon of
'The Times', who had been a great friend of his,
and was also a great friend of my father's.
Landon died in 1927, which is well over half a
century ago. But these verses kept running
through my head after Gott died, so I have quoted
a few lines from them on the dedication page at
the beginning of this book.

This was written in a day when the British owned an Empire on which the sun never set, and could (and did!) regard much of Africa and Asia as their 'Father's house'.

That day has long gone. But whenever I travel eastward to stay with old friends in what was once 'My Father's house' – and mine! – I feel exactly like Kipling did in this poem. Because so much is still there, – the flying fish, the sun and the heat, the boltless doors and the "high-ceiled rooms that the Trade blows through"... Nothing of that has changed.

Kipling's daughter, Elsie was the 'Una' of 'Puck of Pooks Hill' and 'Rewards and Fairies', who I had the good fortune to meet and make friends with while wandering round her father's house, Batemans one day when (this was in the early sixties) the only other visitors had gone out to explore the garden. She took me all over the house and told me that every autumn when the leaves began to fall, the family used to pack up and set off for South Africa, and not come back until the spring. So that it was not until the First World War broke out, and put an end to wintering in the sun, that they discovered that Batemans was one of the coldest houses in Sussex. She said they froze that winter and that her father had been right – "Sirs, it is bitter beneath the Bear!"

SONG OF
THE WISE CHILDREN

When the darkened Fifties dip to the North,
    And frost and the fog divide the air,
And the day is dead at his breaking-forth,
    Sirs, it is bitter beneath the Bear!

Far to Southward they wheel and glance,
    The million molten spears of morn—
The spears of our deliverance
    That shine on the house where we were born.

Flying-fish about our bows,
    Flying sea-fires in our wake:
This is the road to our Father's House,
    Whither we go for our souls' sake!

We have forfeited our birthright,
    We have forsaken all things meet;
We have forgotten the look of light,
    We have forgotten the scent of heat.

They that walk with shaded brows,
    Year by year in a shining land,
They be men of our Father's House,
    They shall receive us and understand.

We shall go back by the boltless doors,
    To the life unaltered our childhood knew—
To the naked feet on the cool, dark floors,
    And the high-ceiled rooms that the Trade
        blows through:

To the trumpet-flowers and the moon beyond,
    And the tree-toad's chorus drowning all—
And the lisp of the split banana-frond
    That talked us to sleep when we were small.

[66]

The wayside magic, the threshold spells,
    Shall soon undo what the North has done—
Because of the sights and the sounds and the smells
    That ran with our youth in the eye of the sun.

And Earth accepting shall ask no vows,
    Nor the Sea our love, nor our lover the Sky.
When we return to our Father's House
    Only the English shall wonder why!

THE PRAYER

My brother kneels, so saith Kabir,
To stone and brass in heathen wise,
But in my brother's voice I hear
My own unanswered agonies.
His God is as his fates assign,
His prayer is all the world's—and mine.

'HARP SONG OF THE DANE WOMEN'

Part Three

—

SEA PIECES

HARP SONG OF
THE DANE WOMEN

What is a woman that you forsake her,
And the hearth-fire and the home-acre,
To go with the old grey Widow-maker?

She has no house to lay a guest in—
But one chill bed for all to rest in,
That the pale suns and the stray bergs nest in.

She has no strong white arms to fold you,
But the ten-times-fingering weed to hold you—
Out on the rocks where the tide has rolled you.

Yet, when the signs of summer thicken,
And the ice breaks, and the birch-buds quicken,
Yearly you turn from our side, and sicken—

Sicken again for the shouts and the slaughters.
You steal away to the lapping waters,
And look at your ship in her winter-quarters.

You forget our mirth, and talk at the tables,
The kine in the shed and the horse in the stables—
To pitch her sides and go over her cables.

Then you drive out where the storm-clouds swallow,
And the sound of your oar-blades, falling hollow,
Is all we have left through the months to follow.

Ah, what is Woman that you forsake her,
And the hearth-fire and the home-acre,
To go with the old grey Widow-maker?

[70]

MINE SWEEPERS

Dawn off the Foreland—the young flood making
   Jumbled and short and steep—
Black in the hollows and bright where it's breaking—
   Awkward water to sweep.
   'Mines reported in the fairway,
   'Warn all traffic and detain.
''Sent up *Unity, Claribel, Assyrian, Stormcock,* and
    Golden Gain.'

Noon off the Foreland—the first ebb making
   Lumpy and strong in the bight.
Boom after boom, and the golf-hut shaking
   And the jackdaws wild with fright!
   'Mines located in the fairway,
   'Boats now working up the chain,
'Sweepers—*Unity, Claribel, Assyrian, Stormcock,* and
    Golden Gain.'

Dusk off the Foreland—the last light going
   And the traffic crowding through,
And five damned trawlers with their syreens blowing
   Heading the whole review!
   'Sweep completed in the fairway.
   'No more mines remain.
''Sent back *Unity, Claribel, Assyrian, Stormcock,* and
    Golden Gain.'

THE DERELICT

'And reports the derelict
Margaret Pollock still at sea.'
—SHIPPING NEWS

I was the staunchest of our fleet
Till the sea rose beneath my feet
Unheralded, in hatred past all measure.
Into his pits he stamped my crew,
Buffeted, blinded, bound and threw,
Bidding me eyeless wait upon his pleasure.

Man made me, and my will
Is to my maker still,
Whom now the currents con, the rollers steer—
Lifting forlorn to spy
Trailed smoke along the sky,
Falling afraid lest any keel come near!

Wrenched as the lips of thirst,
Wried, dried, and split and burst,
Bone-bleached my decks, wind-scoured to the graining;
And, jarred at every roll,
The gear that was my soul
Answers the anguish of my beams' complaining.

For life that crammed me full,
Gangs of the prying gull
That shriek and scrabble on the riven hatches.
For roar that dumbed the gale,
My hawse-pipes' guttering wail,
Sobbing my heart out through the uncounted watches.

Blind in the hot blue ring
Through all my points I swing—
Swing and return to shift the sun anew.
Blind in my well-known sky
I hear the stars go by,
Mocking the prow that cannot hold one true.

[72]

White on my wasted path
Wave after wave in wrath
Frets 'gainst his fellow, warring where to send me.
Flung forward, heaved aside,
Witless and dazed I bide
The mercy of the comber that shall end me.

North where the bergs careen,
The spray of seas unseen
Smokes round my head and freezes in the falling.
South where the corals breed,
The footless, floating weed
Folds me and fouls me, strake on strake upcrawling.

I that was clean to run
My race against the sun—
Strength on the deep—am bawd to all disaster;
Whipped forth by night to meet
My sister's careless feet,
And with a kiss betray her to my master.

Man made me, and my will
Is to my maker still—
To him and his, our peoples at their pier:
Lifting in hope to spy
Trailed smoke along the sky,
Falling afraid lest any keel come near!

Now that we have radar,
I wonder how much
longer we shall have
bell buoys to warn ships
away from unseen
shoals? Will they soon
become a thing of the
past? I hope not. If
only because of these
verses.

THE BELL BUOY

They christened my brother of old—
    And a saintly name he bears—
They gave him his place to hold
    At the head of the belfry-stairs,
    Where the minster-towers stand
And the breeding kestrels cry.
    Would I change with my brother a league inland?
(Shoal! 'Ware shoal!) Not I!

In the flush of the hot June prime,
    O'er sleek flood-tides afire,
I hear him hurry the chime
    To the bidding of checked Desire;
    Till the sweated ringers tire
And the wild bob-majors die.
    Could I wait for my turn in the godly choir?
(Shoal! 'Ware shoal!) Not I!

When the smoking scud is blown—
    When the greasy wind-rack lowers—
Apart and at peace and alone,
    He counts the changeless hours.
    He wars with darkling Powers
(I war with a darkling sea);
    Would he stoop to my work in the gusty mirk?
(Shoal! 'Ware shoal!) Not he!

There was never a priest to pray,
    There was never a hand to toll,
When they made me guard of the bay,
    And moored me over the shoal.
    I rock, I reel, and I roll—
My four great hammers ply—
    Could I speak or be still at the Church's will?
(Shoal! 'Ware shoal!) Not I!

[74]

The landward marks have failed,
    The fog-bank glides unguessed,
The seaward lights are veiled,
    The spent deep feigns her rest:
    But my ear is laid to her breast,
I lift to the swell—I cry!
    Could I wait in sloth on the Church's oath?
(Shoal! 'Ware shoal!) Not I!

At the careless end of night
    I thrill to the nearing screw;
I turn in the clearing light
    And I call to the drowsy crew;
    And the mud boils foul and blue
As the blind bow backs away.
    Will they give me their thanks if they clear the banks?
(Shoal! 'Ware shoal!) Not they!

The beach-pools cake and skim,
    The bursting spray-heads freeze,
I gather on crown and rim
    The grey, grained ice of the seas,
    Where, sheathed from bitt to trees,
The plunging colliers lie.
    Would I barter my place for the Church's grace?
(Shoal! 'Ware shoal!) Not I!

Through the blur of the whirling snow,
    Or the black of the inky sleet,
The lanterns gather and grow,
    And I look for the homeward fleet.
    Rattle of block and sheet—
'Ready about—stand by!'
    Shall I ask them a fee ere they fetch the quay?
(Shoal! 'Ware shoal!) Not I!

I dip and I surge and I swing
    In the rip of the racing tide,

[75]

By the gates of doom I sing,
  On the horns of death I ride.
  A ship-length overside,
Between the course and the sand,
  Fretted and bound I bide
      Peril whereof I cry.
Would I change with my brother a league inland?
(Shoal! 'Ware shoal!) Not I!

THE LAST CHANTEY

'And there was no more sea.'

Thus said the Lord in the Vault above the Cherubim,
  Calling to the Angels and the Souls in their degree:
    'Lo! Earth has passed away
    On the smoke of Judgment Day.
  That Our word may be established shall We gather up
      the sea?'

Loud sang the souls of the jolly, jolly mariners:
  'Plague upon the hurricane that made us furl and flee!
    But the war is done between us,
    In the deep the Lord hath seen us—
  Our bones we'll leave the barracout', and God may sink
      the sea!'

Then said the soul of Judas that betrayèd Him:
  'Lord, hast Thou forgotten Thy covenant with me?
    How once a year I go
    To cool me on the floe?
  And Ye take my day of mercy if Ye take away the sea.'

Then said the soul of the Angel of the Off-shore Wind:
  (He that bits the thunder when the bull-mouthed
      breakers flee):
    'I have watch and ward to keep
    O'er Thy wonders on the deep,
  And Ye take mine honour from me if Ye take away the sea!'

Loud sang the souls of the jolly, jolly mariners:
  'Nay, but we were angry, and a hasty folk are we.
    If we worked the ship together
    Till she foundered in foul weather,
  Are we babes that we should clamour for a vengeance on
      the sea?'

[77]

A favourite verse. I have always liked the idea of those ancient mariners making a hash of playing their golden harps, when their only previous experience of sing-songs would probably have been bawling chanteys in bad weather, or singing rude songs in the pub!

Then said the souls of the slaves that men threw overboard:
   'Kennelled in the picaroon a weary band were we;
     But Thy arm was strong to save,
     And it touched us on the wave,
   And we drowsed the long tides idle till Thy Trumpets tore
      the sea.'

Then cried the soul of the stout Apostle Paul to God:
   'Once we frapped a ship, and she laboured woundily.
     There were fourteen score of these,
     And they blessed Thee on their knees,
   When they learned Thy Grace and Glory under Malta by
      the sea!'

Loud sang the souls of the jolly, jolly mariners,
   Plucking at their harps, and they plucked unhandily:
     'Our thumbs are rough and tarred,
     And the tune is something hard—
   May we lift a Deepsea Chantey such as seamen use at sea?'

Then said the souls of the gentlemen-adventurers—
   Fettered wrist to bar all for red iniquity:
     'Ho, we revel in our chains
     O'er the sorrow that was Spain's!
   Heave or sink it, leave or drink it, we were masters of
      the sea!'

Up spake the soul of a grey Gothavn 'speckshioner—
   (He that led the flenching in the fleets of fair Dundee):
     'Oh, the ice-blink white and near,
     And the bowhead breaching clear!
   Will Ye whelm them all for wantonness that wallow in
      the sea?'

[78]

Loud sang the souls of the jolly, jolly mariners,
　　Crying: 'Under Heaven, here is neither lead nor lee!
　　　Must we sing for evermore
　　　On the windless, glassy floor?
　　Take back your golden fiddles and we'll beat to open sea!'

Then stooped the Lord, and He called the good sea up to Him,
　　And 'stablishèd its borders until all eternity,
　　　That such as have no pleasure
　　　For to praise the Lord by measure,
　　They may enter into galleons and serve Him on the sea.

Sun, Wind, and Cloud shall fail not from the face of it,
　　Stinging, ringing spindrift, nor the fulmar flying free;
　　　And the ships shall go abroad
　　　To the Glory of the Lord
　　Who heard the silly sailor-folk and gave them back their sea!

Tacklow and Kipling had a close mutual friend – The same Percival Landon
to whose memory, Kipling wrote 'A song in The Desert'.
Discussing R.K's methods one day, Landon said Rudyard went to
enormous pains over detail and did his best never to make
a mistake.
"He made one in 'The Last Chantey'," said Tacklow, "because the only
whale that doesn't breach" (leap out of the water) "is the bowhead!"
Months later, Landon wrote to say that he told Kipling this, and that
R.K had checked and was dismayed to find that it was so, and
wanted to know what he had better do about it?
Tacklow replied suggesting that he should follow the sterling example
of the well-known author, William Le Quex, who wrote under
the pseudonym of 'Q'. (see Troy Town, etc). In the second edition
of his book, 'Dead Man's Rock', 'Q' added a brief preface that read:
"Since the publication of this book, at least five hundred people who
have no better use for their time have written to me to point out
that Bombay is not on the Bay of Bengal. I would like to point out
that for the purposes of this story Bombay is, and will remain, on
the Bay of Bengal". Kipling, according to Landon, was delighted
with this retort and laughed his head off. Though I don't suppose he
ever made any use of it.
(That quote, by the way, is from memory, and as I do not possess a
second edition of 'Dead Man's Rock', I merely give the _muttab_ of it!)
Muttab is a useful Hindustani word meaning 'general sense of'.

[79]

'MY BOY JACK'

Part Four

WAR POEMS

Naked and grey the Cotswolds stand
    Beneath the autumn sun,
And the stubble-fields on either hand
    Where Stour and Avon run.
There is no change in the patient land
    That has bred us every one.

She should have passed in cloud and fire
    And saved us from this sin
Of war—red war—'twixt child and sire,
    Household and kith and kin,
In the heart of a sleepy Midland shire,
    With the harvest scarcely in.

But there is no change as we meet at last
    On the brow-head or the plain,
And the raw astonished ranks stand fast
    To slay or to be slain
By the men they knew in the kindly past
    That shall never come again—

By the men they met at dance or chase,
    In the tavern or the hall,
At the justice-bench and the market-place,
    At the cudgel-play or brawl—
Of their own blood and speech and race,
    Comrades or neighbours all!

More bitter than death this day must prove
    Whichever way it go,
For the brothers of the maids we love
    Make ready to lay low
Their sisters' sweethearts, as we move
    Against our dearest foe.

Thank Heaven! At last the trumpets peal
  Before our strength gives way.
For King or for the Commonweal—
  No matter which they say,
The first dry rattle of new-drawn steel
  Changes the world to-day!

These verses could just as easily have been written about the American Civil War — or any Civil War. In fact the battle of Edgehill saw the opening shots of the bitter struggle between the Cavaliers and the Roundheads — the royalists who supported King Charles I, and the forces of his Parliament who had risen in revolt against him under the leadership of Oliver Cromwell.

It was the first battle in a Civil War that was to divide the country and very many families, setting brother against brother and father against son, and it was a bloody, chaotic an inconclusive mêlée. By sunset, when both sides fell back to the positions they had taken up at dawn, the bodies of five thousand dead and wounded fellow-countrymen littered the stubble fields, and it is said that the Vicar of Kineton, a little Cotswold village where Cromwell's men had based their baggage-train, buried twelve hundred dead in the course of the next few days. Many of them were men who had played together from infancy, been to school together, and known each other all their lives.

Though written before the turn of the century, these verses might almost have been written for the Indian and Gurkha regiments who fought alongside the British in the First World War: as they did in the Second. The men who knelt at different altars—

HYMN BEFORE ACTION

The earth is full of anger,
    The seas are dark with wrath,
The Nations in their harness
    Go up against our path:
Ere yet we loose the legions—
    Ere yet we draw the blade,
Jehovah of the Thunders,
    Lord God of Battles, aid!

High lust and froward bearing,
    Proud heart, rebellious brow—
Deaf ear and soul uncaring,
    We seek Thy mercy now!
The sinner that forswore Thee,
    The fool that passed Thee by,
Our times are known before Thee—
    Lord, grant us strength to die!

For those who kneel beside us
    At altars not Thine own,
Who lack the lights that guide us,
    Lord, let their faith atone!
If wrong we did to call them,
    By honour bound they came;
Let not Thy Wrath befall them,
    But deal to us the blame.

From panic, pride, and terror,
    Revenge that knows no rein—
Light haste and lawless error,
    Protect us yet again.
Cloke Thou our undeserving,
    Make firm the shuddering breath,
In silence and unswerving
    To taste Thy lesser death.

[84]

Ah, Mary pierced with sorrow,
　　Remember, reach and save
The soul that comes to-morrow
　　Before the God that gave!
Since each was born of woman,
　　For each at utter need—
True comrade and true foeman—
　　Madonna, intercede!

E'en now their vanguard gathers,
　　E'en now we face the fray—
As Thou didst help our fathers,
　　Help Thou our host to-day.
Fulfilled of signs and wonders,
　　In life, in death made clear—
Jehovah of the Thunders,
　　Lord God of Battles, hear!

The peace-at-any-price pacifists would probably object to this prayer. But in time of war every Believer prays to his or her own God, and this is how most if not all of us would pray.

Anyone who read Ernest Hemingway's novel about the Spanish Civil War, 'For Whom the Bell Tolls', will not have forgotten how the young and dedicated communist, who hated the Church and its priests and did not believe in God, hears the drone of the approaching bombers, and suddenly realising he is about to die, falls on his knees and begins to pray to the Virgin — as he was taught to do as a child.

In times of crisis we surely all pray. This is not a war-monger or a 'jingo' speaking. This is someone praying for the 'true foeman' as well as true comrades.

LICHTENBERG

Smells are surer than sounds or sights
　　To make your heart-strings crack—
They start those awful voices o' nights
　　That whisper, 'Old man, come back!'
That must be why the big things pass
　　And the little things remain,
Like the smell of the wattle by Lichtenberg,
　　Riding in, in the rain.

There was some silly fire on the flank
　　And the small wet drizzling down—
There were the sold-out shops and the bank
　　And the wet, wide-open town;
And we were doing escort-duty
　　To somebody's baggage-train,
And I smelt wattle by Lichtenberg—
　　Riding in, in the rain.

It was all Australia to me—
　　All I had found or missed:
Every face I was crazy to see,
　　And every woman I'd kissed:
All that I shouldn't ha' done, God knows!
　　(As He knows I'll do it again),
That smell of the wattle round Lichtenberg,
　　Riding in, in the rain!

And I saw Sydney the same as ever,
　　The picnics and brass-bands;
And my little homestead on Hunter River
　　And my new vines joining hands.
It all came over me in one act
　　Quick as a shot through the brain—
With the smell of the wattle round Lichtenberg,
　　Riding in, in the rain.

[86]

I have forgotten a hundred fights,
    But one I shall not forget—
With the raindrops bunging up my sights
    And my eyes bunged up with wet;
And through the crack and the stink of the cordite,
    (Ah, Christ! My country again!)
The smell of the wattle by Lichtenberg,
    Riding in, in the rain!

In 1900, after The Boer War had broken out, Kipling went out to South Africa and found Cape Town awash with newspaper correspondents (This is how he first met Percival Landon of 'The Times').

Within a day or two he was caught up in his old profession and was eventually co-opted by General Roberts – Lord Roberts of Kandahar, a fellow Anglo-Indian – to help launch an army newspaper in Bloemfontein.

Australian troops had joined Roberts' army, and it must have been one of them who told R.K about catching a whiff of the familiar scent of wattle flowers as an Australian contingent rode into Lichtenberg in the rain.

Oh, how quickly a scent or a tune can take you back in time: I don't know which is more potent. The scent of Cosmos in bloom conjures up Simla for me; sweet peas in the sun sends me back to my garden in Kohat. And whenever I smell iris's – which don't really have a scent, only the smell of spring – I am once more driving down the long road that leads through the Valley of Kashmir to Srinagar, in a twilight that is full of the scent of iris. That is why I love these verses; because I know how that Australian felt.

[87]

This is one of R.K's
Boer War poems.
Written in memory
of the hospital
nurses who volunteered
for service in South
Africa, and died there
of disease and
overwork.

Mary Kingsley, a family
friend, was one of them.
She had volunteered
to nurse in a
prisoner-of-war
camp in Simon's Town
during an epidemic
of typhoid, where she
caught the disease
and died of it.

Who recalls the twilight and the rangèd tents in order
    (Violet peaks uplifted through the crystal evening air?)
And the clink of iron teacups and the piteous, noble laughter,
    And the faces of the Sisters with the dust upon their hair?

(Now and not hereafter, while the breath is in our nostrils,
    Now and not hereafter, ere the meaner years go by—
Let us now remember many honourable women,
    Such as bade us turn again when we were like to die.)

Who recalls the morning and the thunder through the foot-hills,
    (Tufts of fleecy shrapnel strung along the empty plains?)
And the sun-scarred Red-Cross coaches creeping guarded to
       the culvert,
    And the faces of the Sisters looking gravely from the trains?

(When the days were torment and the nights were clouded
       terror,
    When the Powers of Darkness had dominion on our soul—
When we fled consuming through the Seven Hells of Fever,
    These put out their hands to us and healed and made us
       whole.)

Who recalls the midnight by the bridge's wrecked abutment,
    (Autumn rain that rattled like a Maxim on the tin?)
And the lightning-dazzled levels and the streaming, straining
       wagons,
    And the faces of the Sisters as they bore the wounded in?

(Till the pain was merciful and stunned us into silence—
    When each nerve cried out to God that made the misused clay;
When the Body triumphed and the last poor shame departed—
    These abode our agonies and wiped the sweat away.)

[88]

Who recalls the noontide and the funerals through the market,
  (Blanket-hidden bodies, flagless, followed by the flies?)
And the footsore firing-party, and the dust and stench and
      staleness,
  And the faces of the Sisters and the glory in their eyes?

(Bold behind the battle, in the open camp all-hallowed,
  Patient, wise, and mirthful in the ringed and reeking town,
These endured unresting till they rested from their labours—
  Little wasted bodies, ah, so light to lower down!)

Yet their graves are scattered and their names are clean
      forgotten,
  Earth shall not remember, but the Waiting Angel knows
Them that died at Uitvlugt when the plague was on the city—
  Her that fell at Simon's Town[1] in service on our foes.

Wherefore we they ransomed, while the breath is in our nostrils,
  Now and not hereafter—ere the meaner years go by—
Praise with love and worship many honourable women,
  Those that gave their lives for us when we were like to die!

[1]Mary Kingsley

[89]

*Mary Kingsley (1862–1900) Biologist
and Botanist. Author of 'Travels
in West Africa' and once described
as 'the cleverest of the famous
Victorian women travellers'.*

EPITAPHS OF THE WAR

A SON

My son was killed while laughing at some jest.
                    I would I knew
What it was, and it might serve me in a time
                    when jests are few.

EX-CLERK

Pity not! The Army gave
Freedom to a timid slave:
In which Freedom did he find
Strength of body, will, and mind:
By which strength he came to prove
Mirth, Companionship, and Love:
For which Love to Death he went:
In which Death he lies content.

HINDU SEPOY IN FRANCE

This man in his own country prayed we know not to
                    what Powers.
We pray Them to reward him for his bravery in ours.

PELICANS IN THE WILDERNESS

'A Grave near Halfa'

The blown sand heaps on me, that none may learn
        Where I am laid for whom my children grieve. . .
O wings that beat at dawning, ye return
        Out of the desert to your young at eve!

COMMON FORM

If any question why we died,
Tell them, because our fathers lied.

THE FAVOUR

Death favoured me from the first, well knowing I could not endure
To wait on him day by day. He quitted my betters and came
Whistling over the fields, and, when he had made all sure,
'Thy line is at end,' he said, 'but at least I have saved its name.'

BATTERIES OUT OF AMMUNITION

If any mourn us in the workshop, say
We died because the shift kept holiday.

CONVOY ESCORT

I was a shepherd to fools
   Causelessly bold or afraid.
They would not abide by my rules.
   Yet they escaped. For I stayed.

SALONIKAN GRAVE

I have watched a thousand days
Push out and crawl into night
Slowly as tortoises.
Now I, too, follow these.
It is fever, and not the fight—
Time, not battle,—that slays.

ACTORS

We counterfeited once for your disport
   Men's joy and sorrow: but our day has passed.
We pray you pardon all where we fell short—
   Seeing we were your servants to this last.

This epitaph is engraved on a memorial tablet in Holy Trinity Church, Stratford-on-Avon.

JOURNALISTS

We have served our day.

And this one on a panel in the Hall of The Institute of Journalists.

[91]

The entire population of
Great Britain was issued
with gas masks when
World War II broke out
in 1939. But the effects
of gas in the First World
War had been so
appalling that no nation
could face being the first
to use it again.
It was about the only
weapon not used
during the last war. It
is therefore not reassuring
to learn that several
nations in the near and
far East are busy
stockpiling the beastly stuff.

GETHSEMANE

The Garden called Gethsemane
   In Picardy it was,
And there the people came to see
   The English soldiers pass.
We used to pass—we used to pass
   Or halt, as it might be,
And ship our masks in case of gas
   Beyond Gethsemane.

The Garden called Gethsemane,
   It held a pretty lass,
But all the time she talked to me
   I prayed my cup might pass.
The officer sat on the chair,
   The men lay on the grass,
And all the time we halted there
   I prayed my cup might pass.

It didn't pass—it didn't pass—
   It didn't pass from me.
I drank it when we met the gas
   Beyond Gethsemane!

MY BOY JACK

'Have you news of my boy Jack?'
  Not this tide.
'When d'you think that he'll come back?'
  Not with this wind blowing, and this tide.

'Has any one else had word of him?'
  Not this tide.
For what is sunk will hardly swim,
  Not with this wind blowing, and this tide.

'Oh, dear, what comfort can I find?'
  None this tide,
  Nor any tide,
Except he did not shame his kind—
  Not even with that wind blowing, and that tide.

Then hold your head up all the more,
  This tide,
  And every tide;
Because he was the son you bore,
  And gave to that wind blowing and that tide!

The great Naval battles
of the first World War
cost an appalling
number of lives, and
The bodies of those
who die at sea are
seldom recovered.
Thousands of people
must have asked
for news of a boy They
would never see
again. Kipling among
Them: Though his boy
was in the army—

[93]

R.K warned again and again about the coming of the First World War in speeches articles and verses. But no one wanted to know or listen, and all he got for his pains was to be accused of being a 'war-monger'.

When it came, his country was hopelessly unprepared; and it was left to a small volunteer army 'the Old Contemptibles', and untrained civilians who rushed to enlist, to bear the brunt and die for their country's mistakes.

These were our children who died for our lands: they
were dear in our sight.
We have only the memory left of their home-treasured
sayings and laughter.
The price of our loss shall be paid to our hands, not
another's hereafter.
Neither the Alien nor Priest shall decide on it. That is our
right.
But who shall return us the children?

At the hour the Barbarian chose to disclose his pretences,
And raged against Man, they engaged, on the breasts
that they bared for us,
The first felon-stroke of the sword he had long-time
prepared for us—
Their bodies were all our defence while we wrought our
defences.

They bought us anew with their blood, forbearing to
blame us,
Those hours which we had not made good when the
Judgment o'ercame us.
They believed us and perished for it. Our statecraft, our
learning
Delivered them bound to the Pit and alive to the burning
Whither they mirthfully hastened as jostling for honour—
Not since her birth has our Earth seen such worth loosed
upon her.

Nor was their agony brief, or once only imposed on them.
  The wounded, the war-spent, the sick received no
    exemption:
  Being cured they returned and endured and achieved
    our redemption,
Hopeless themselves of relief, till Death, marvelling,
    closed on them.

That flesh we had nursed from the first in all cleanness
    was given
To corruption unveiled and assailed by the malice of
    Heaven—
By the heart-shaking jests of Decay where it lolled on the
    wires—
To be blanched or gay-painted by fumes—to be cindered
    by fires—
To be senselessly tossed and retossed in stale mutilation
From crater to crater. For this we shall take expiation.
  But who shall return us our children?

Kipling's only son, John, was one of the twenty thousand British dead who fell in the terrible, inconclusive Battle of Loos in the second year of the First World War.

His body was never found and his name is listed on the Menin Gate among those who have no known grave.

He spent his last leave at his home in Sussex, from where he left for France on his eighteenth birthday; looking, said his mother, "very smart and straight and young and brave"

She was never to see him again.
Poor Carrie!

'FOLLOW ME 'OME'

There was no one like 'im, 'Orse or Foot,
    Nor any o' the Guns I knew;
An' because it was so, why, o' course 'e went an' died,
    Which is just what the best men do.

So it's knock out your pipes an' follow me!
An' it's finish up your swipes an' follow me!
    Oh, 'ark to the big drum callin',
      Follow me—follow me 'ome!

'Is mare she neighs the 'ole day long,
    She paws the 'ole night through,
An' she won't take 'er feed 'cause o' waitin' for 'is step,
    Which is just what a beast would do.

'Is girl she goes with a bombardier
    Before 'er month is through;
An' the banns are up in church, for she's got the beggar hooked,
    Which is just what a girl would do.

We fought 'bout a dog—last week it were—
    No more than a round or two;
But I strook 'im cruel 'ard, an' I wish I 'adn't now,
    Which is just what a man can't do.

'E was all that I 'ad in the way of a friend,
    An' I've 'ad to find one new;
But I'd give my pay an' stripe for to get the beggar back,
    Which it's just too late to do!

So it's knock out your pipes an' follow me!
An' it's finish up your swipes an' follow me!
    Oh, 'ark to the fifes a-crawlin'!
      Follow me—follow me 'ome!

Take 'im away! 'E's gone where the best men go.
Take 'im away! An' the gun-wheels turnin' slow.
Take 'im away! There's more from the place 'e come.
Take 'im away, with the limber an' the drum.

    For it's 'Three rounds blank' an' follow me,
    An' it's 'Thirteen rank' an' follow me;
      Oh, passin' the love o' women,
        Follow me—follow me 'ome!

R.K always picks exactly the right word.
The pipes at a military funeral do crawl:
you feel them right down your spine.

I would have liked to have asked him why,
when he dropped the H's from 'ome, 'orse,
'im etc, he made an exception of 'hooked'?
Did he think that the unenlightened
foreigner wouldn't be able to translate
'ooked' because, in the way he has used
it here, it is slang?
It's a trivial point. But he must have had
a good reason for keeping in that H——

[97]

REBIRTH

If any God should say,
  'I will restore
The world her yesterday
  Whole as before
My Judgment blasted it'—who would not lift
Heart, eye, and hand in passion o'er the gift?

If any God should will
  To wipe from mind
The memory of this ill
  Which is mankind
In soul and substance now—who would not bless
Even to tears His loving-tenderness?

If any God should give
  Us leave to fly
These present deaths we live,
  And safely die
In those lost lives we lived ere we were born—
What man but would not laugh the excuse to scorn?

For we are what we are—
  So broke to blood
And the strict works of war—
  So long subdued
To sacrifice, that threadbare Death commands
Hardly observance at our busier hands.

Yet we were what we were,
  And, fashioned so,
It pleases us to stare
  At the far show
Of unbelievable years and shapes that flit,
In our own likeness, on the edge of it.

*Well, what would you
say given the choice?
Any takers?*

[98]

THE STORM CONE

This is the midnight—let no star
Delude us—dawn is very far.
This is the tempest long foretold—
Slow to make head but sure to hold.

Stand by! The lull 'twixt blast and blast
Signals the storm is near, not past;
And worse than present jeopardy
May our forlorn to-morrow be.

If we have cleared the expectant reef,
Let no man look for his relief.
Only the darkness hides the shape
Of further peril to escape.

It is decreed that we abide
The weight of gale against the tide
And those huge waves the outer main
Sends in to set us back again.

They fall and whelm. We strain to hear
The pulses of her labouring gear,
Till the deep throb beneath us proves,
'After each shudder and check, she moves!

She moves, with all save purpose lost,
To make her offing from the coast;
But, till she fetches open sea,
Let no man deem that he is free!

I have always believed that Kipling had a crystal ball in his head and that he forsaw the Second World War: as he had foreseen the first.
This was written at a time when everyone was saying gaily that Hitler wouldn't dream of starting a war, and that he wasn't doing a bad job putting Germany on her feet, etc, etc, and that this was just the same old Kipling, yelling 'Fire!'

Now I see that someone is determined to make out that this was only Kipling playing party-politics, so there! Pity.

[99]

Part Five

—

PHILOSOPHY

Many of those who have written about Kipling have expressed doubts as to his religious beliefs, and seem to think that he was probably an agnostic. Though how any agnostic could have written these verses, and many others not included in this book, I don't know.

Nor do I believe that any 'unbeliever' could have said, back in the 1890's after the death of his best friend, Wolcott Balestier, "we had so much to say to each other, and now I have to wait so long before I can say it."
He wasn't given to telling lies, polite or otherwise.
He meant that. And nor does he seem to have changed his mind during the last days of his life.

'MY NEW-CUT ASHLAR'

My new-cut ashlar takes the light
Where crimson-blank the windows flare.
By my own work before the night,
Great Overseer, I make my prayer.

If there be good in that I wrought
Thy Hand compelled it, Master, Thine—
Where I have failed to meet Thy Thought
I know, through Thee, the blame was mine.

One instant's toil to Thee denied
Stands all Eternity's offence.
Of that I did with Thee to guide,
To Thee, through Thee, be excellence.

The depth and dream of my desire,
The bitter paths wherein I stray—
Thou knowest Who hast made the Fire,
Thou knowest Who hast made the Clay.

Who, lest all thought of Eden fade,
Bring'st Eden to the craftsman's brain—
Godlike to muse o'er his own Trade
And manlike stand with God again!

One stone the more swings into place
In that dread Temple of Thy worth.
It is enough that, through Thy Grace,
I saw nought common on Thy Earth.

Take not that vision from my ken—
Oh, whatsoe'er may spoil or speed.
Help me to need no aid from men
That I may help such men as need!

A SONG TO MITHRAS
Hymn of the XXX Legion: circa AD 350

Mithras, God of the Morning, our trumpets waken the Wall!
'Rome is above the Nations, but Thou art over all!'
Now as the names are answered, and the guards are marched away,
Mithras, also a soldier, give us strength for the day!

Mithras, God of the Noontide, the heather swims in the heat.
Our helmets scorch our foreheads, our sandals burn our feet.
Now in the ungirt hour—now lest we blink and drowse,
Mithras, also a soldier, keep us true to our vows!

Mithras, God of the Sunset, low on the Western main—
Thou descending immortal, immortal to rise again!
Now when the watch is ended, now when the wine is drawn,
Mithras, also a soldier, keep us pure till the dawn!

Mithras, God of the Midnight, here where the great Bull dies,
Look on Thy children in darkness. Oh, take our sacrifice!
Many roads Thou hast fashioned—all of them lead to the Light!
Mithras, also a soldier, teach us to die aright!

In the days when Rome ruled most of the
known world, Mithras was the soldiers' god,
and the sacred rites that accompanied
his worship included the killing of a bull.

[103]

I read these verses long
before I ever dreamed
That I would one day
visit Japan. And when
I did so, I was even
more fortunate,
for the Japan I saw
was still very much
like the country that
the young Kipling saw.
And for the last time.
The very last—!

There was only one
European hotel in
'Nikko the beautiful,
where the Shōguns
sleep', and no railway
between Nikko and
Lake Chuzenji.
Japanese men still
wore the traditional
grey robes—though
there was a sinister
tendancy to add
a homberg hat to the
outfit!—and their
women were adorable:
gay-sashed and
beautifully coloured
butterflies.
If you saw one
wearing western dress,
you turned to stare.

Oh dear! All that is
ended. And at
Kamakura only the
great Buddha
remains the same.
For World War II was
lying in wait just
around the corner,
and when it leapt out
of the shadows, old
Japan vanished in
the crash of guns
and bombs.

BUDDHA AT KAMAKURA

'And there is a Japanese idol at Kamakura.'

O ye who tread the Narrow Way
By Tophet-flare to Judgment Day,
Be gentle when 'the heathen' pray
    To Buddha at Kamakura!

To Him the Way, the Law, apart,
Whom Maya held beneath her heart,
Ananda's Lord, the Bodhisat,
    The Buddha of Kamakura.

For though he neither burns nor sees,
Nor hears ye thank your Deities,
Ye have not sinned with such as these,
    His children at Kamakura,

Yet spare us still the Western joke
When joss-sticks turn to scented smoke
The little sins of little folk
    That worship at Kamakura—

The grey-robed, gay-sashed butterflies
That flit beneath the Master's eyes.
He is beyond the Mysteries
    But loves them at Kamakura.

And whoso will, from Pride released,
Contemning neither creed nor priest,
May feel the Soul of all the East
    About him at Kamakura.

Yea, every tale Ananda heard,
Of birth as fish or beast or bird,
While yet in lives the Master stirred,
    The warm wind brings Kamakura.

[104]

Till drowsy eyelids seem to see.
A-flower 'neath her golden *htee*
The Shwe-Dagon flare easterly
   From Burma to Kamakura,

And down the loaded air there comes
The thunder of Thibetan drums,
And droned—*'Om mane padme hum's'*[1]
   A world's-width from Kamakura.

Yet Brahmans rule Benares still,
Buddh-Gaya's ruins pit the hill,
And beef-fed zealots threaten ill
   To Buddha and Kamakura.

A tourist-show, a legend told,
A rusting bulk of bronze and gold,
So much, and scarce so much, ye hold
   The meaning of Kamakura?

But when the morning prayer is prayed,
Think, ere ye pass to strife and trade,
Is God in human image made
   No nearer than Kamakura?

Kipling saw the Buddha in 1889, and I can only suppose that at that time Kamakura was pronounced 'Ka-makura'. Because that scans: 'Kama-kura' doesn't! Perhaps someone can tell me about that.

[1] The Buddhist invocation

[105]

All over the great land that was once, for a brief space of time, British India, and that is now two countries, India and Pakistan, you will find deserted places of worship. Forlorn and crumbling churches, temples and mosques that were left behind by the departing legions of 'the Raj', or by Hindus or Muslims—refugees fleeing for their lives before the senseless holocaust that followed the decision to partition the sub-continent.

Any building in which believers have prayed for a hundred years and more —much more, in the case of temples and mosques —cannot help but aquire a special feeling of holiness. So it is sad to see such places crumbling and desolate like the deserted shrine in this poem. Perhaps one day 'some deity on wandering wing' will pause for a while to be worshipped there, but I doubt it. It seems to me more likely that they will be left to disintegrate until the little - the very little - that still remains visible, can no longer be regarded as consecrated ground. And when that happens the speculators and their bulldozers will move in, and another office block or tourist hotel will arise on the spot where the long dead generations once prayed to their God.
'Then shall the dust return to earth as it was...

L'ENVOI
to *Departmental Ditties*

The smoke upon your Altar dies,
   The flowers decay,
The Goddess of your sacrifice
   Has flown away.
What profit then to sing or slay
The sacrifice from day to day?

'We know the Shrine is void,' they said,
   'The Goddess flown—
'Yet wreaths are on the altar laid—
   'The Altar-Stone
'Is black with fumes of sacrifice,
'Albeit She has fled our eyes.

'For, it may be, if still we sing
   'And tend the Shrine,
'Some Deity on wandering wing
   'May there incline;
'And, finding all in order meet,
'Stay while we worship at Her feet.'

'BY THE HOOF
OF THE WILD GOAT'

By the Hoof of the Wild Goat uptossed
From the cliff where she lay in the Sun
Fell the Stone
To the Tarn where the daylight is lost,
So she fell from the light of the Sun
And alone!

Now the fall was ordained from the first
With the Goat and the Cliff and the Tarn,
But the Stone
Knows only her life is accursed
As she sinks from the light of the Sun
And alone!

O Thou Who has builded the World,
O Thou Who hast lighted the Sun,
O Thou Who hast darkened the Tarn,
Judge Thou
The sin of the Stone that was hurled
By the goat from the light of the Sun,
As she sinks in the mire of the Tarn,
Even now—even now—even now!

'What is written is written'...

I wish I knew what was
in Kipling's mind when
he wrote this poem.
Was he putting into verse
the Muslim theory that one's
fate is 'tied about one's
neck' and cannot be
avoided? If so, it was
certainly not something
that he himself believed.
So what was he thinking?

This is only one of
several of his verses that
I love but do not
understand. 'Gethsemene'
is another. And so is
'cold Iron', which I have
not included in this book.

The verses stick in my
head and I would give
a lot to know what was
in his. I have, of course,
like everyone else who
reads them, my own
ideas as to what he
was after.
But how many of us
are right?

[107]

THE DISCIPLE

He that hath a Gospel
　　To loose upon Mankind,
Though he serve it utterly—
　　Body, soul and mind—
Though he go to Calvary
　　Daily for its gain—
It is His Disciple
　　Shall make his labour vain.

He that hath a Gospel
　　For all earth to own—
Though he etch it on the steel,
　　Or carve it on the stone—
Not to be misdoubted
　　Through the after-days—
It is His Disciple
　　Shall read it many ways.

It is His Disciple
　　(Ere Those Bones are dust)
Who shall change the Charter,
　　Who shall split the Trust—
Amplify distinctions,
　　Rationalise the Claim;
Preaching that the Master
　　Would have done the same.

It is His Disciple
　　Who shall tell us how
Much the Master would have scrapped
　　Had he lived till now—
What he would have modified
　　Of what he said before.
It is His Disciple
　　Shall do this and more . . .

[108]

He that hath a Gospel
   Whereby Heaven is won
(Carpenter, or cameleer,
   Or Maya's dreaming son),
Many swords shall pierce Him,
   Mingling blood with gall;
But His Own Disciple
   Shall wound Him worst of all!

These verses must make sense to anyone who has seen the tawdry, tinsel trimmings and exotic rituals that have been added down the centuries to any number of gospels that were originally simple and uncluttered.

What must the Carpenter's Son think of the ornate chapels and squabbling sects in Christian Jerusalem? Or 'Maya's dreaming son' of the elaborate Devil Dances in the courtyards of his monasteries in Tibet?

Or, for that matter, what must the ghost of Karl Marx think of the power and splendour of the fat cats who live in the Kremlin and drive around in Rolls Royces and private aeroplanes?

[109]

Tacklow, my father—who was on leave and in London at the time of Queen Victoria's second Jubilee, the 'Diamond Jubilee' of 1897—and who stood in the crowd on Ludgate Hill to see her drive past, told me that an enormous amount of fulsome verse and grandiloquent prose was written and published in honour of the occasion. Including, he said, a particularly sugar and milk effusion by the Poet Laureate, Alfred Austin. And then, suddenly, when the whole thing was over and the celebrations had petered out leaving everyone feeling remarkably pleased, smug and self-satisfied, and preening themselves on being British and ruling half the world, The Times' printed 'Recessional'...

He said I could have no idea of the impact it made—coming on top of all that boastful back-slapping and showing off. Like a jug of cold water dashed in the face of a yelling, capering drunk. It sobered up everyone who read it, and brought them down to earth. Yet even then it seemed the carpers and the critics got busy and started on the usual nit-picking of the bandur-log. The forerunners of today's rabid 'anti-racist' nit-pickers, screeching that 'lesser breeds without the law' was a crack against all coloured people. Which in itself is a 'racist' remark in that it assumes no white race could be called a 'lesser breed' or be 'lawless'. Oh can't they! You don't have to be coloured to be a 'heathen'—or white to be a Christian.

RECESSIONAL

God of our fathers, known of old,
   Lord of our far-flung battle-line,
Beneath whose awful hand we hold
   Dominion over palm and pine—
Lord God of Hosts, be with us yet,
Lest we forget—lest we forget!

The tumult and the shouting dies;
   The Captains and the Kings depart:
Still stands Thine ancient sacrifice,
   An humble and a contrite heart.
Lord God of Hosts, be with us yet,
Lest we forget—lest we forget!

Far-called, our navies melt away;
   On dune and headland sinks the fire:
Lo, all our pomp of yesterday
   Is one with Nineveh and Tyre!
Judge of the Nations, spare us yet,
Lest we forget—lest we forget!

If, drunk with sight of power, we loose
   Wild tongues that have not Thee in awe,
Such boastings as the Gentiles use,
   Or lesser breeds without the Law—
Lord God of Hosts, be with us yet,
Lest we forget—lest we forget!

For heathen heart that puts her trust
   In reeking tube and iron shard,
All valiant dust that builds on dust,
   And guarding, calls not Thee to guard,
For frantic boast and foolish word—
Thy mercy on Thy People, Lord!

THE PALACE

When I was a King and a Mason—a Master proven and skilled—
I cleared me ground for a Palace such as a King should build.
I decreed and dug down to my levels. Presently, under the silt,
I came on the wreck of a Palace such as a King had built.

There was no worth in the fashion—there was no wit in the plan—
Hither and thither, aimless, the ruined footings ran—
Masonry, brute, mishandled, but carven on every stone:
'After me cometh a Builder. Tell him, I too have known.'

Swift to my use in my trenches, where my well-planned ground-
    works grew,
I tumbled his quoins and his ashlars, and cut and reset them anew.
Lime I milled of his marbles; burned it, slacked it, and spread;
Taking and leaving at pleasure the gifts of the humble dead.

Yet I despised not nor gloried; yet, as we wrenched them apart,
I read in the razed foundations the heart of that builder's heart.
As he had risen and pleaded, so did I understand
The form of the dream he had followed in the face of the thing he
    had planned.

  .   .   .   .

When I was a King and a Mason—in the open noon of my pride,
They sent me a Word from the Darkness. They whispered and
    called me aside.
They said—'The end is forbidden.' They said—'Thy use is
    fulfilled.
'Thy Palace shall stand as that other's—the spoil of a King who
    shall build.'
I called my men from my trenches, my quarries, my wharves,
    and my sheers.
All I had wrought I abandoned to the faith of the faithless years.
Only I cut on the timber—only I carved on the stone:
'After me cometh a Builder. Tell him, I too have known!'

[111]

EDDI'S SERVICE

Eddi, priest of St. Wilfrid
   In his chapel at Manhood End,
Ordered a midnight service
   For such as cared to attend.

But the Saxons were keeping Christmas,
   And the night was stormy as well.
Nobody came to service
   Though Eddi rang the bell.

''Wicked weather for walking,'
   Said Eddi of Manhood End.
'But I must go on with the service
   For such as care to attend.'

The altar-lamps were lighted, —
   An old marsh-donkey came,
Bold as a guest invited,
   And stared at the guttering flame.

The storm beat on at the windows,
   The water splashed on the floor,
And a wet, yoke-weary bullock
   Pushed in through the open door.

'How do I know what is greatest,
   How do I know what is least?
That is My Father's business,'
   Said Eddi, Wilfrid's priest.

'But—three are gathered together—
   Listen to me and attend.
I bring good news, my brethren!'
   Said Eddi of Manhood End.

[112]

And he told the Ox of a Manger
  And a Stall in Bethlehem,
And he spoke to the Ass of a Rider
  That rode to Jerusalem.

They steamed and dripped in the chancel,
  They listened and never stirred,
While, just as though they were Bishops,
  Eddi preached them The Word,

Till the gale blew off on the marshes
  And the windows showed the day,
And the Ox and Ass together
  Wheeled and clattered away.

And when the Saxons mocked him,
  Said Eddi of Manhood End,
'I dare not shut His chapel
  On such as care to attend.'

PRIMITIVE

I ate my fill of a whale that died
　　And stranded after a month at sea. . .
There is a pain in my inside.
　　Why have the Gods afflicted me?
Ow! I am purged till I am a wraith!
　　Wow! I am sick till I cannot see!
What is the sense of Religion and Faith?
　　Look how the Gods have afflicted me!

PAGAN

How can the skin of rat or mouse hold
　　Anything more than a harmless flea? . . .
The burning plague has taken my household.
　　Why have my Gods afflicted me?
All my kith and kin are deceased,
　　Though they were as good as good could be.
I will out and batter the family priest,
　　Because my Gods have afflicted me!

MEDIÆVAL

My privy and well drain into each other
　　After the custom of Christendie. . .
Fevers and fluxes are wasting my mother.
　　Why has the Lord afflicted me?
The Saints are helpless for all I offer—
　　So are the clergy I used to fee.
Henceforward I keep my cash in my coffer,
　　Because the Lord has afflicted me.

MATERIAL

I run eight hundred hens to the acre.
   They die by dozens mysteriously. . .
I am more than doubtful concerning my Maker.
   Why has the Lord afflicted me?
What a return for all my endeavour—
   Not to mention the L.S.D.!
I am an atheist now and for ever,
   Because this God has afflicted me!

PROGRESSIVE

Money spent on an Army or Fleet
   Is homicidal lunacy. . .
My son has been killed in the Mons retreat.
   Why is the Lord afflicting me?
Why are murder, pillage and arson
   And rape allowed by the Deity?
I will write to the *Times*, deriding our parson,
   Because my God has afflicted me.

CHORUS

We had a kettle: we let it leak:
   Our not repairing it made it worse.
We haven't had any tea for a week. . .
   The bottom is out of the Universe!

CONCLUSION

This was none of the good Lord's pleasure,
   For the Spirit He breathed in Man is free;
But what comes after is measure for measure
   And not a God that afflicteth thee.
As was the sowing so the reaping
   Is now and evermore shall be.
Thou art delivered to thine own keeping.
   Only Thyself hath afflicted thee!

If anyone should think this attitude is out of date, I would just like to mention that only a year or two ago, someone I know well declared furiously that he was not going to attend his Parish Church again, because a gale that had arisen the previous night had stripped off the tarpaulin and plastic-sheeting that had been protecting the ceilings of the upper storey of his house while the roof was being repaired: thus letting in the rain.

Since this was presumably an 'Act of God', he was damned if he would continue to observe the Sabbath — so there!

[115]

'THE SONG OF DIEGO VALDEZ'

Part Six

———

VARIOUS VERSES

I used to think of these verses whenever I saw 'Staff College Hill' in Berlin, in the days when Gott was commanding the Berlin Brigade in the British sector of that divided city.

The hill, which rose above the skyline of what was still, at that time, a ruined city, was always referred to by the British army as Staff College Hill because a great many staff college exercises started with the words: "Take an imaginary hill.." — or town or lake or whatever. And this hill in Berlin was not a real one. It was still in the process of construction and we used to watch the steady stream of lorries winding up to deposit their loads of rubble; rubble that had once been Berlin. For this hill was being formed out of the broken pieces of homes, shops, churches, offices, hospitals and colleges, and grandiose blocks of municiple buildings. Hitler's Berlin.

Watching it grow it was impossible not to wonder what a generation of archaeologists far in the future would make of it as they dug in the rubble of that 'spent and unconsidered earth'.

'CITIES AND THRONES AND POWERS'

Cities and Thrones and Powers
   Stand in Time's eye,
Almost as long as flowers,
   Which daily die:
But, as new buds put forth
   To glad new men,
Out of the spent and unconsidered Earth
   The Cities rise again.

This season's Daffodil,
   She never hears
What change, what chance, what chill,
   Cut down last year's;
But with bold countenance,
   And knowledge small,
Esteems her seven days' continuance
   To be perpetual.

So Time that is o'er-kind
   To all that be,
Ordains us e'en as blind,
   As bold as she:
That in our very death,
   And burial sure,
Shadow to shadow, well persuaded, saith,
   'See how our works endure!'

[118]

DANE-GELD

It is always a temptation to an armed and agile nation
    To call upon a neighbour and to say:—
'We invaded you last night—we are quite prepared to fight,
    Unless you pay us cash to go away.'

And that is called asking for Dane-geld,
    And the people who ask it explain
That you've only to pay 'em the Dane-geld
    And then you'll get rid of the Dane!

It is always a temptation to a rich and lazy nation,
    To puff and look important and to say:—
'Though we know we should defeat you, we have not the
        time to meet you.
    We will therefore pay you cash to go away.'

And that is called paying the Dane-geld;
    But we've proved it again and again,
That if once you have paid him the Dane-geld
    You never get rid of the Dane.

It is wrong to put temptation in the path of any nation,
    For fear they should succumb and go astray;
So when you are requested to pay up or be molested,
    You will find it better policy to say:—

'We never pay *any*-one Dane-geld,
    No matter how trifling the cost;
For the end of that game is oppression and shame,
    And the nation that plays it is lost!'

'Dane-Geld' was the original Protection-Money racket. It was demanded of the Britons in the years after Rome withdrew her legions and left the country wide open to invasion by sea-raiders from the North; Danes Saxons, Vikings. It was money demanded by the raiders in return for a promise to leave without doing any damage and not to come again. Once it was paid, the Danes, having spent it, came for more — upping the ante each time. They never kept their bargain. Why should they? It was a splendidly easy way of getting rich quick.

We need to remember this, in these days of hi-jackers and kidnappers, all of them demanding millions in cash or military hardware for ransome.

Sooner or later we are going to have to learn that last verse of Dane-Geld by heart, and say it at the top of our voices. And prove that we mean it!

[119]

PUCK'S SONG

See you the ferny ride that steals
Into the oak-woods far?
O that was whence they hewed the keels
That rolled to Trafalgar.

And mark you where the ivy clings
To Bayham's mouldering walls?
O there we cast the stout railings
That stand around St. Paul's.

See you the dimpled track that runs
All hollow through the wheat?
O that was where they hauled the guns
That smote King Philip's fleet.

(Out of the Weald, the secret Weald,
Men sent in ancient years
The horse-shoes red at Flodden Field,
The arrows at Poitiers!)

See you our little mill that clacks,
So busy by the brook?
She has ground her corn and paid her tax
Ever since Domesday Book.

See you our stilly woods of oak,
And the dread ditch beside?
O that was where the Saxons broke
On the day that Harold died.

See you the windy levels spread
About the gates of Rye?
O that was where the Northmen fled,
When Alfred's ships came by.

See you our pastures wide and lone,
Where the red oxen browse?
O there was a City thronged and known,
Ere London boasted a house.

And see you, after rain, the trace
Of mound and ditch and wall?
O that was a Legion's camping-place,
When Caesar sailed from Gaul.

And see you marks that show and fade,
Like shadows on the Downs?
O they are the lines the Flint Men made,
To guard their wondrous towns.

Trackway and Camp and City lost,
Salt Marsh where now is corn—
Old Wars, old Peace, old Arts that cease,
And so was England born!

She is not any common Earth,
Water or wood or air,
But Merlin's Isle of Gramarye,
Where you and I will fare!

Our house was in Sussex. Only a few miles, as the crow flies, from Kipling's home, Batemans, and no distance at all from Battle, where the Battle of Hastings was fought in 1066, and William the Bastard, Duke of Normandy — William the Conquerer — defeated King Harold and his Saxons and later built the great Abbey of Battle in celebration of his victory.

That fight changed the course of history, and the ground on which it was fought is much the same now as it was then.

Many of our friends would come down from London to have lunch and spend the day with us, and since our nearest station was Battle, Gott would meet them there and drive them to the Old House.
He liked to stop on the way and show them where Harold and his House Carles had stood, and where William's forces had taken up their position and launched their attack.
He was as fascinated by the history of Sussex as Kipling had been.

THE BENEFACTORS

Ah! What avails the classic bent
*   And what the cultured word,*
Against the undoctored incident
*   That actually occurred?*

And what is Art whereto we press
*   Through paint and prose and rhyme—*
When Nature in her nakedness
*   Defeats us every time?*

It is not learning, grace nor gear,
    Nor easy meat and drink,
But bitter pinch of pain and fear
    That makes creation think.

When in this world's unpleasing youth
    Our godlike race began,
The longest arm, the sharpest tooth,
    Gave man control of man;

Till, bruised and bitten to the bone
    And taught by pain and fear,
He learned to deal the far-off stone,
    And poke the long, safe spear.

So tooth and nail were obsolete
    As means against a foe,
Till, bored by uniform defeat,
    Some genius built the bow.

Then stone and javelin proved as vain
    As old-time tooth and nail;
Till, spurred anew by fear and pain,
    Man fashioned coats of mail.

Then there was safety for the rich
   And danger for the poor,
Till someone mixed a powder which
   Redressed the scale once more.

Helmet and armour disappeared
   With sword and bow and pike,
And, when the smoke of battle cleared,
   All men were armed alike . . .

And when ten million such were slain
   To please one crazy king,
Man, schooled in bulk by fear and pain,
   Grew weary of the thing;

And, at the very hour designed
   To enslave him past recall,
His tooth-stone-arrow-gun-shy mind
   Turned and abolished all.

All Power, each Tyrant, every Mob
   Whose head has grown too large,
Ends by destroying its own job
   And works its own discharge;

And Man, whose mere necessities
   Move all things from his path,
Trembles meanwhile at their decrees,
   And deprecates their wrath!

Hail Progress! These verses
seem to me as relevant now
as they were when Kipling
wrote them.
In fact (when you come to
think of it), even more so
now than then!

[123]

MERROW DOWN

I

There runs a road by Merrow Down—
    A grassy track to-day it is—
An hour out of Guildford town,
    Above the river Wey it is.

Here, when they heard the horse-bells ring,
    The ancient Britons dressed and rode ˙
To watch the dark Phœnicians bring
    Their goods along the Western Road.

Yes, here, or hereabouts, they met
    To hold their racial talks and such—
To barter beads for Whitby jet,
    And tin for gay shell torques and such.

But long and long before that time
    (When bison used to roam on it)
Did Taffy and her Daddy climb
    That Down, and had their home on it.

Then beavers built in Broadstonebrook
    And made a swamp where Bramley stands;
And bears from Shere would come and look
    For Taffimai where Shamley stands.

The Wey, that Taffy called Wagai,
    Was more than six times bigger then;
And all the Tribe of Tegumai
    They cut a noble figure then!

II

Of all the Tribe of Tegumai
    Who cut that figure, none remain,—
On Merrow Down the cuckoos cry—
    The silence and the sun remain.

[124]

But as the faithful years return
   And hearts unwounded sing again,
Comes Taffy dancing through the fern
   To lead the Surrey spring again.

Her brows are bound with bracken-fronds,
   And golden elf-locks fly above;
Her eyes are bright as diamonds
   And bluer than the sky above.

In mocassins and deer-skin cloak,
   Unfearing, free and fair she flits,
And lights her little damp-wood smoke
   To show her Daddy where she flits.

For far—oh, very far behind,
   So far she cannot call to him,
Comes Tegumai alone to find
   The daughter that was all to him!

JOSEPHINE

from a photograph.
'The daughter who was
all to him!'

[125]

THE ROMAN CENTURION'S SONG

Legate, I had the news last night—my cohort ordered home
By ship to Portus Itius and thence by road to Rome.
I've marched the companies aboard, the arms are stowed below:
Now let another take my sword. Command me not to go!

I've served in Britain forty years, from Vectis to the Wall.
I have none other home than this, nor any life at all.
Last night I did not understand, but, now the hour draws near
That calls me to my native land, I feel that land is here.

Here where men say my name was made, here where my work
        was done;
Here where my dearest dead are laid—my wife—my wife and
        son;
Here where time, custom, grief and toil, age, memory, service,
        love,
Have rooted me in British soil. Ah, how can I remove?

For me this land, that sea, these airs, those folk and fields
        suffice.
What purple Southern pomp can match our changeful Northern
        skies,
Black with December snows unshed or pearled with August
        haze—
The clanging arch of steel-grey March, or June's long-lighted
        days?

You'll follow widening Rhodanus till vine and olive lean
Aslant before the sunny breeze that sweeps Nemausus clean
To Arelate's triple gate; but let me linger on,
Here where our stiff-necked British oaks confront Euroclydon!

You'll take the old Aurelian Road through shore-descending
     pines
Where, blue as any peacock's neck, the Tyrrhene Ocean
     shines.
You'll go where laurel crowns are won, but—will you e'er
     forget
The scent of hawthorn in the sun, or bracken in the wet?

Let me work here for Britain's sake—at any task you will—
A marsh to drain, a road to make or native troops to drill.
Some Western camp (I know the Pict) or granite Border keep,
Mid seas of heather derelict, where our old messmates sleep.

Legate, I come to you in tears—My cohort ordered home!
I've served in Britain forty years. What should I do in Rome?
Here is my heart, my soul, my mind—the only life I know.
I cannot leave it all behind. Command me not to go!

These verses tell of one of the major trip-wires attached to aquiring an
Empire. People grow fond of the countries in which their working
lives are spent.
The speaker here could just as easily be an Anglo-Indian, many of
whom, when the time came for them to retire and leave the land in
which they had served for the greater part of their lives, found it
hard to face the prospect of ending their days in one that had
become strange to them. Some of these opted instead for Staying On,
which did not always work. Particularly after Independence.

THE SONG
OF DIEGO VALDEZ

The God of Fair Beginnings
    Hath prospered here my hand—
The cargoes of my lading,
    And the keels of my command.
For out of many ventures
    That sailed with hope as high,
My own have made the better trade,
    And Admiral am I.

To me my King's much honour,
    To me my people's love—
To me the pride of Princes
    And power all pride above;
To me the shouting cities,
    To me the mob's refrain:—
'Who knows not noble Valdez
    'Hath never heard of Spain.'

But I remember comrades—
    Old playmates on new seas—
Whenas we traded orpiment
    Among the savages—
A thousand leagues to south'ard
    And thirty years removed—
They knew not noble Valdez,
    But me they knew and loved.

Then they that found good liquor,
    They drank it not alone,
And they that found fair plunder,
    They told us every one,
About our chosen islands
    Or secret shoals between,
When, weary from far voyage,
    We gathered to careen.

[128]

There burned our breaming-fagots
  All pale along the shore:
There rose our worn pavilions—
  A sail above an oar:
As flashed each yearning anchor
  Through mellow seas afire,
So swift our careless captains
  Rowed each to his desire.

Where lay our loosened harness?
  Where turned our naked feet?
Whose tavern 'mid the palm-trees?
  What quenchings of what heat?
Oh, fountain in the desert!
  Oh, cistern in the waste!
Oh, bread we ate in secret!
  Oh, cup we spilled in haste!

The youth new-taught of longing,
  The widow curbed and wan,
The goodwife proud at season,
  And the maid aware of man—
All souls unslaked, consuming,
  Defrauded in delays,
Desire not more their quittance
  Than I those forfeit days!

I dreamed to wait my pleasure
  Unchanged my spring would bide:
Wherefore, to wait my pleasure,
  I put my spring aside
Till, first in face of Fortune,
  And last in mazed disdain,
I made Diego Valdez
  High Admiral of Spain.

Then walked no wind 'neath Heaven
  Nor surge that did not aid—

I dared extreme occasion,
     Nor ever one betrayed.
They wrought a deeper treason—
     (Led seas that served my needs!)
They sold Diego Valdez
     To bondage of great deeds.

The tempest flung me seaward,
     And pinned and bade me hold
The course I might not alter—
     And men esteemed me bold!
The calms embayed my quarry,
     The fog-wreath sealed his eyes;
The dawn-wind brought my topsails—
     And men esteemed me wise!

Yet,'spite my tyrant triumphs,
     Bewildered, dispossessed—
My dream held I before me—
     My vision of my rest;
But, crowned by Fleet and People,
     And bound by King and Pope—
Stands here Diego Valdez
     To rob me of my hope.

No prayer of mine shall move him.
     No word of his set free
The Lord of Sixty Pennants
     And the Steward of the Sea.
His will can loose ten thousand
     To seek their loves again—
But not Diego Valdez,
     High Admiral of Spain.

There walks no wind 'neath Heaven
     Nor wave that shall restore
The old careening riot
     And the clamorous, crowded shore—

The fountain in the desert,
    The cistern in the waste,
The bread we ate in secret,
    The cup we spilled in haste.

Now call I to my Captains—
    For council fly the sign—
Now leap their zealous galleys,
    Twelve-oared, across the brine.
To me the straiter prison,
    To me the heavier chain—
To me Diego Valdez,
    High Admiral of Spain!

Is Kipling thinking of himself as Diego Valdez, I wonder? Longing for the old days of 'Fair Beginnings', and realising sadly that those carefree days are gone for ever, and that he has sold himself 'to bondage of great deeds'— and Carrie? Maybe!

'THE WAY THROUGH THE WOODS'

THE WAY
THROUGH THE WOODS

They shut the road through the woods
Seventy years ago.
Weather and rain have undone it again,
And now you would never know
There was once a road through the woods
Before they planted the trees.
It is underneath the coppice and heath
And the thin anemones.
Only the keeper sees
That, where the ring-dove broods,
And the badgers roll at ease,
There was once a road through the woods.

Yet, if you enter the woods
Of a summer evening late,
When the night-air cools on the trout-ringed pools
Where the otter whistles his mate,
(They fear not men in the woods,
Because they see so few.)
You will hear the beat of a horse's feet,
And the swish of a skirt in the dew,
Steadily cantering through
The misty solitudes,
As though they perfectly knew
The old lost road through the woods . . .
But there is no road through the woods.

THE CRAFTSMAN

Once, after long-drawn revel at The Mermaid,
He to the overbearing Boanerges
Jonson, uttered (if half of it were liquor,
    Blessed be the vintage!)

Saying how, at an alehouse under Cotswold,
He had made sure of his very Cleopatra
Drunk with enormous, salvation-contemning
    Love for a tinker.

How, while he hid from Sir Thomas's keepers,
Crouched in a ditch and drenched by the midnight
Dews, he had listened to gypsy Juliet
    Rail at the dawning.

How at Bankside, a boy drowning kittens
Winced at the business; whereupon his sister—
Lady Macbeth aged seven—thrust 'em under,
    Sombrely scornful.

How on a Sabbath, hushed and compassionate—
She being known since her birth to the townsfolk—
Stratford dredged and delivered from Avon
    Dripping Ophelia.

So, with a thin third finger marrying
Drop to wine-drop domed on the table,
Shakespeare opened his heart till the sunrise
    Entered to hear him.

London waked and he, imperturbable,
Passed from waking to hurry after shadows . . .
Busied upon shows of no earthly importance?
    Yes, but he knew it!

[135]

This is R.K's idea of how Shakespeare collected ideas for his plays, and it was probably true.
It was certainly how Kipling came up with his 'notions'; and how Somerset-Maugham, for one, got the material for his short stories.

This isn't the only poem he wrote on this subject. The other one is called 'The Coiner', but it is not in this book. It tells how Shakespeare could have acquired the plot of 'The Tempest'.

A St. Helena Lullaby

'How far is St. Helena from a little child at play?'
What makes you want to wander there with all the world
        between?
Oh, Mother, call your son again or else he'll run away.
(No one thinks of winter when the grass is green!)

'How far is St. Helena from a fight in Paris Street?'
I haven't time to answer now—the men are falling fast.
The guns begin to thunder, and the drums begin to beat.
(If you take the first step, you will take the last!)

'How far is St. Helena from the field of Austerlitz?'
You couldn't hear me if I told—so loud the cannon roar.
But not so far for people who are living by their wits.
('Gay go up' means 'Gay go down' the wide world o'er!)

'How far is St. Helena from an Emperor of France?'
I cannot see—I cannot tell—the Crowns they dazzle so.
The Kings sit down to dinner, and the Queens stand up
        to dance.
(After open weather you may look for snow!)

'How far is St. Helena from the Capes of Trafalgar?'
A longish way—a longish way—with ten year more to run.
It's South across the water underneath a falling star.
(What you cannot finish you must leave undone!)

'How far is St. Helena from the Beresina ice?'
An ill way—a chill way—the ice begins to crack.
But not so far for gentlemen who never took advice.
(When you can't go forward you must e'en come back!)

[136]

'How far is St. Helena from the field of Waterloo?'
A near way—a clear way—the ship will take you soon.
A pleasant place for gentlemen with little left to do.
(Morning never tries you till the afternoon!)

'How far from St. Helena to the Gate of Heaven's Grace?'
That no one knows—that no one knows—and no one ever will.
But fold your hands across your heart and cover up your face,
And after all your trapesings, child, lie still!

Father, Mother, and Me,
    Sister and Auntie say
All the people like us are We,
    And everyone else is They.
And They live over the sea,
    While We live over the way,
But—would you believe it?—They look upon We
    As only a sort of They!

We eat pork and beef
    With cow-horn-handled knives.
They who gobble Their rice off a leaf,
    Are horrified out of Their lives;
While They who live up a tree,
    And feast on grubs and clay,
(Isn't it scandalous?) look upon We
    As a simply disgusting They!

We shoot birds with a gun.
    They stick lions with spears.
Their full-dress is un-.
    We dress up to Our ears.
They like Their friends for tea.
    We like Our friends to stay;
And, after all that, They look upon We
    As an utterly ignorant They!

We eat kitcheny food.
    We have doors that latch.
They drink milk or blood,
    Under an open thatch.
We have Doctors to fee.
    They have Wizards to pay.
And (impudent heathen!) They look upon We
    As a quite impossible They!

[138]

All good people agree,
     And all good people say,
All nice people, like Us, are We
     And every one else is They:
But if you cross over the sea,
     Instead of over the way,
You may end by (think of it!) looking on We
     As only a sort of They!

A great many of Us are also convinced that THEY all look so alike that we can't tell one from the other. I presume THEY think the same about US?

When we were living in North China, in a house in Peking, Tacklow, (who spoke Chinese fluently, both Mandarin and Cantonese), talking one day with a Chinese friend of his, was suprised to see that another and elderly Chinaman, who was present, was holding his nose. When the old man left, Tacklow enquired why he should have done this. His friend was embarrassed: "You must excuse him. He is only a peasant and knows no better".

"Yes, but why did he do it?" asked my father, interested.

"Well, if you must know", confessed his friend, "all you Europeans smell so unpleasant,—but it was very bad manners to behave like that!"

Tacklow was fascinated! It seems that, to the Chinese, Europeans smell of the food they eat— too much red meat I suppose?— and of soap and cigarettes and, possibly alcohol and coffee?

The combination, to a Chinaman is unpleasant. And WE all thought THEY had an odd smell! (All that cooking oil!) Oh well—!

[139]

A TRUTHFUL SONG

THE BRICKLAYER:

I tell this tale, which is strictly true,
Just by way of convincing you
How very little, since things were made,
Things have altered in the building trade.

A year ago, come the middle of March,
We was building flats near the Marble Arch,
When a thin young man with coal-black hair
Came up to watch us working there.

Now there wasn't a trick in brick or stone
Which this young man hadn't seen or known;
Nor there wasn't a tool from trowel to maul
But this young man could use 'em all!

Then up and spoke the plumbyers bold,
Which was laying the pipes for the hot and cold:
'Since you with us have made so free,
Will you kindly say what your name might be?'

The young man kindly answered them:
'It might be Lot or Methusalem,
Or it might be Moses (a man I hate),
Whereas it is Pharaoh surnamed the Great.

'Your glazing is new and your plumbing's strange,
But otherwise I perceive no change;
And in less than a month if you do as I bid
I'd learn you to build me a Pyramid!'

THE SAILOR:

I tell this tale, which is stricter true,
Just by way of convincing you
How very little, since things was made,
Things have altered in the shipwright's trade.

[140]

In Blackwall Basin yesterday
A China barque re-fitting lay,
When a fat old man with snow-white hair
Came up to watch us working there.

Now there wasn't a knot which the riggers knew
But the old man made it—and better too;
Nor there wasn't a sheet, or a lift, or a brace,
But the old man knew its lead and place.

Then up and spoke the caulkyers bold,
Which was packing the pump in the afterhold:
'Since you with us have made so free,
Will you kindly tell what your name might be?'

The old man kindly answered them:
'It might be Japheth, it might be Shem,
Or it might be Ham (though his skin was dark),
Whereas it is Noah, commanding the Ark.

'Your wheel is new and your pumps are strange,
But otherwise I perceive no change;
And in less than a week, if she did not ground,
I'd sail this hooker the wide world round!'

BOTH:
We tell these tales, which are strictest true,
Just by way of convincing you
How very little, since things was made,
Anything alters in any one's trade!

I wonder how many of our modern inventions would have surprised Leonardo da Vinci? Not many, I'll bet!

[141]

'Farewell, Romance!' the Cave-men said;
  'With bone well carved He went away.
'Flint arms the ignoble arrowhead,
  'And jasper tips the spear to-day.
'Changed are the Gods of Hunt and Dance,
'And He with these. Farewell, Romance!'

'Farewell, Romance!' the Lake-folk sighed;
  'We lift the weight of flatling years;
'The caverns of the mountain-side
  'Hold Him who scorns our hutted piers.
'Lost hills whereby we dare not dwell,
'Guard ye His rest. Romance, Farewell!'

'Farewell, Romance!' the Soldier spoke;
  'By sleight of sword we may not win,
'But scuffle 'mid uncleanly smoke
  'Of arquebus and culverin.
'Honour is lost, and none may tell
'Who paid good blows. Romance, farewell!'

'Farewell, Romance!' the Traders cried;
  'Our keels have lain with every sea.
'The dull-returning wind and tide
  'Heave up the wharf where we would be;
'The known and noted breezes swell
'Our trudging sails. Romance, farewell!'

'Good-bye, Romance!' the Skipper said;
  'He vanished with the coal we burn.
'Our dial marks full-steam ahead,
  'Our speed is timed to half a turn.
'Sure as the ferried barge we ply
''Twixt port and port. Romance, good-bye!'

[142]

'Romance!' the season-tickets mourn,
    '*He* never ran to catch His train,
'But passed with coach and guard and horn—
    'And left the local—late again!
'Confound Romance!'. . . And all unseen
Romance brought up the nine-fifteen.

His hand was on the lever laid,
    His oil-can soothed the worrying cranks,
His whistle waked the snowbound grade,
    His fog-horn cut the reeking Banks;
By dock and deep and mine and mill
The Boy-god reckless laboured still!

Robed, crowned and throned, He wove His spell,
    Where heart-blood beat or hearth-smoke curled,
With unconsidered miracle,
    Hedged in a backward-gazing world:
Then taught His chosen bard to say:
'Our King was with us—yesterday!'

That particular King will always
'be with us— yesterday'
Why is it that the past always
looks so much better than
the present?

Will we look back one day with
nostalgia at Concorde and the
Jumbo-jet?

'TOMLINSON' RUDYARD KIPLING

I am charmed to see that George Sharp has drawn Tomlinson's
Devil as Oscar Wilde. Very appropriate! for I have no doubt
that in Tomlinson's day many Victorians, including Their Queen,
regarded poor Oscar as Lucifer's deputy, if not Lucifer himself,
and Tomlinson would not have been in the least surprised to
find Hell looking like an over-heated brothel, with Oscar Wilde
in charge — and enjoying himself!

TOMLINSON

Now Tomlinson gave up the ghost at his house in Berkeley
      Square,
And a Spirit came to his bedside and gripped him by the
      hair—
A Spirit gripped him by the hair and carried him far away,
Till he heard as the roar of a rain-fed ford the roar of the
      Milky Way:
Till he heard the roar of the Milky Way die down and drone
      and cease,
And they came to the Gate within the Wall where Peter
      holds the keys.
'Stand up, stand up now, Tomlinson, and answer loud and
      high
'The good that ye did for the sake of men or ever ye came
      to die—
'The good that ye did for the sake of men on little Earth so
      lone!'
And the naked soul of Tomlinson grew white as a rain-
      washed bone.
'O I have a friend on Earth,' he said, 'that was my priest
      and guide,
'And well would he answer all for me if he were at my
      side.'
—'For that ye strove in neighbour-love it shall be written
      fair,
'But now ye wait at Heaven's Gate and not in Berkeley
      Square:
'Though we called your friend from his bed this night, he
      could not speak for you,
'For the race is run by one and one never by two and two.'
Then Tomlinson looked up and down, and little gain was
      there,
For the naked stars grinned overhead, and he saw that his
      soul was bare.
The Wind that blows between the Worlds, it cut him like a
      knife,

[145]

And Tomlinson took up the tale and spoke of his good in
    life.
'O this I have read in a book,' he said, 'and that was told to
    me,
'And this I have thought that another man thought of a
    Prince in Muscovy.'
The good souls flocked like homing doves and bade him
    clear the path,
And Peter twirled the jangling Keys in weariness and
    wrath.
'Ye have read, ye have heard, ye have thought,' he said,
    'and the tale is yet to run:
'By the worth of the body that·once ye had, give answer—
    what ha' ye done?'
Then Tomlinson looked back and forth, and little good it
    bore,
For the darkness stayed at his shoulder-blade and
    Heaven's Gate before:—
'O this I have felt, and this I have guessed, and this I have
    heard men say,
'And this they wrote that another man wrote of a carl in
    Norroway.'
'Ye have read, ye have felt, ye have guessed, good lack!
    Ye have hampered Heaven's Gate;
'There's little room between the stars in idleness to prate!
'For none may reach by hired speech of neighbour, priest,
    and kin
'Through borrowed deed to God's good meed that lies so
    fair within;
'Get hence, get hence to the Lord of Wrong, for the doom
    has yet to run,
'And . . . the faith that ye share with Berkeley Square
    uphold you, Tomlinson!'

       ·   ·   ·   ·   ·   ·   ·   ·

The Spirit gripped him by the hair, and sun by sun they fell
Till they came to the belt of Naughty Stars that rim the
    mouth of Hell.

[146]

The first are red with pride and wrath, the next are white
with pain,
But the third are black with clinkered sin that cannot burn
again.
They may hold their path, they may leave their path, with
never a soul to mark:
They may burn or freeze, but they must not cease in the
Scorn of the Outer Dark.
The Wind that blows between the Worlds, it nipped him to
the bone,
And he yearned to the flare of Hell-gate there as the light
of his own hearth-stone.
The Devil he sat behind the bars, where the desperate
legions drew,
But he caught the hasting Tomlinson and would not let him
through.
'Wot ye the price of good pit-coal that I must pay?' said he,
'That ye rank yoursel' so fit for Hell and ask no leave of
me?
'I am all o'er-sib to Adam's breed that ye should give me
scorn,
'For I strove with God for your First Father the day that
he was born.
'Sit down, sit down upon the slag, and answer loud and
high
'The harm that ye did to the Sons of Men or ever you
came to die.'
And Tomlinson looked up and up, and saw against the
night
The belly of a tortured star blood-red in Hell-Mouth light;
And Tomlinson looked down and down, and saw beneath
his feet
The frontlet of a tortured star milk-white in Hell-Mouth
heat.
'O I had a love on earth,' said he, 'that kissed me to my
fall;
'And if ye would call my love to me I know she would
answer all.'

[147]

We liked The idea of
The Devil having
to buy his 'good pit
coal', and used to
wonder who
he bought it from?

Presumably someone
on one of the
'Naughty' Stars. A red
one, naturally,
since the white ones
would not have any
to spare, and the
black ones were
burned out.

—'All that ye did in love forbid it shall be written fair,
'But now ye wait at Hell-Mouth Gate and not in Berkeley
      Square:
'Though we whistled your love from her bed to-night, I
      trow she would not run,
'For the sin ye do by two and two ye must pay for one by
      one!'
The Wind that blows between the Worlds, it cut him like a
      knife,
And Tomlinson took up the tale and spoke of his sins in
      life:—
'Once I ha' laughed at the power of Love and twice at the
      grip of the Grave,
'And thrice I ha' patted my God on the head that men
      might call me brave.'
The Devil he blew on a brandered soul and set it aside to
      cool:—
'Do ye think I would waste my good pit-coal on the hide of
      a brain-sick fool?
'I see no worth in the hobnailed mirth or the jolthead jest
      ye did
'That I should waken my gentlemen that are sleeping
      three on a grid.'
Then Tomlinson looked back and forth, and there was
      little grace,
For Hell-Gate filled the houseless soul with the Fear of
      Naked Space.
'Nay, this I ha' heard,' quo' Tomlinson, 'and this was
      noised abroad,
'And this I ha' got from a Belgian book on the word of a
      dead French lord.'
—'Ye ha' heard, ye ha' read, ye ha' got, good lack! and the
      tale begins afresh—
'Have ye sinned one sin for the pride o' the eye or the
      sinful lust of the flesh?'
Then Tomlinson he gripped the bars and yammered, 'Let
      me in—

I thought of
"Tomlinson" when I
saw the first moon-
landing on T.V.
That bleached
landscape against
the blackness of
empty space—'the
Scorn of the Outer
Dark'. And I
wondered if the men
inside those clumsy
space-suits had
ever been afraid,
as Tomlinson had
been, 'with the Fear
of Naked Space'.
The appalling
loneliness of it.....

'For I mind that I borrowed my neighbour's wife to sin the
       deadly sin.'
The Devil he grinned behind the bars, and banked the
       fires high:
'Did ye read of that sin in a book?' said he; and Tomlinson
       said, 'Ay!'
The Devil he blew upon his nails, and the little devils ran,
And he said: 'Go husk this whimpering thief that comes in
       the guise of a man:
'Winnow him out 'twixt star and star, and sieve his proper
       worth:
'There's sore decline in Adam's line if this be spawn of
       Earth.'
Empusa's crew, so naked-new they may not face the fire,
But weep that they bin too small to sin to the height of
       their desire,
Over the coal they chased the Soul, and racked it all
       abroad,
As children rifle a caddis-case or the raven's foolish hoard.
And back they came with the tattered Thing, as children
       after play,
And they said: 'The soul that he got from God he has
       bartered clean away.
'We have threshed a stook of print and book, and
       winnowed a chattering wind,
'And many a soul wherefrom he stole, but his we cannot
       find.
'We have handled him, we have dandled him, we have
       seared him to the bone,
'And, Sire, if tooth and nail show truth he has no soul of his
       own.'
The Devil he bowed his head on his breast and rumbled
       deep and low:—
'I'm all o'er-sib to Adam's breed that I should bid him go.
'Yet close we lie, and deep we lie, and if I gave him place,
'My gentlemen that are so proud would flout me to my
       face;

'They'd call my house a common stews and me a careless
     host,
'And—I would not anger my gentlemen for the sake of a
     shiftless ghost.'
The Devil he looked at the mangled Soul that prayed to
     feel the flame,
And he thought of Holy Charity, but he thought of his own
     good name:—
'Now ye could haste my coal to waste, and sit ye down to
     fry.
'Did ye think of that theft for yourself?' said he; and
     Tomlinson said, 'Ay!'
The Devil he blew an outward breath, for his heart was
     free from care:—
'Ye have scarce the soul of a louse,' he said, 'but the roots
     of sin are there,
'And for that sin should ye come in were I the lord alone,
'But sinful pride has rule inside—ay, mightier than my
     own.
'Honour and Wit, fore-damned they sit, to each his Priest
     and Whore;
'Nay, scarce I dare myself go there, and you they'd
     torture sore.
'Ye are neither spirit nor spirk,' he said; 'ye are neither
     book nor brute—
'Go, get ye back to the flesh again for the sake of Man's
     repute.
'I'm all o'er-sib to Adam's breed that I should mock your
     pain,
'But look that ye win to worthier sin ere ye come back
     again.
'Get hence, the hearse is at your door—the grim black
     stallions wait—
'They bear your clay to place to-day. Speed, lest ye come
     too late!
'Go back to Earth with a lip unsealed—go back with an
     open eye,

*He wasn't given
much of a margin,
was he! for if
The hearse was at
The door he ought
to have been
in his coffin.
I suppose he came
back and sat up
just as They were
going to put The
lid on.*

*I've often wondered
in Which place he
eventually ended
up. Upstairs? or
Down?*

[150]

'And carry my word to the Sons of Men or ever ye come
      to die:
'That the sin they do by two and two they must pay for
      one by one,
'And . . . the God that you took from a printed book be
      with you, Tomlinson!'

Kipling always admired doers: craftsmen, workers who, whatever the work, knew what they were doing and did it well.

If he had a motto it might well have been 'Whatsoever thy hand findeth to do, do it with all thy might.'

A man like Tomlinson would have been anathema to him, and I am sure he modelled the Tomlinson in these verses on someone he knew.
A rich nonentity without an ounce of character. A 'Kutch-nai' in fact – which is Hindustani for 'nothing'.

A SONG OF TRAVEL

Where's the lamp that Hero lit
    Once to call Leander home?
Equal Time hath shovelled it
    'Neath the wrack of Greece and Rome.
Neither wait we any more
That worn sail which Argo bore.

Dust and dust of ashes close
    All the Vestal Virgins' care;
And the oldest altar shows
    But an older darkness there.
Age-encamped Oblivion
Tenteth every light that shone.

Yet shall we, for Suns that die,
    Wall our wanderings from desire?
Or, because the Moon is high,
    Scorn to use a nearer fire?
Lest some envious Pharaoh stir,
Make our lives our sepulchre?

Nay! Though Time with petty Fate
    Prison us and Emperors,
By our Arts do we create
    That which Time himself devours—
Such machines as well may run
'Gainst the Horses of the Sun.

When we would a new abode,
    Space, our tyrant King no more,
Lays the long lance of the road
    At our feet and flees before,
Breathless, ere we overwhelm,
To submit a further realm!

[152]

THE GODS OF
THE COPYBOOK HEADINGS

As I pass through my incarnations in every age and race,
I make my proper prostrations to the gods of the Market-
Place.
Peering through reverent fingers I watch them flourish
and fall,
And the Gods of the Copybook Headings, I notice, outlast
them all.

We were living in trees when they met us. They showed
us each in turn
That Water would certainly wet us, as Fire would certainly
burn:
But we found them lacking in Uplift, Vision and Breadth of
Mind,
So we left them to teach the Gorillas while we followed
the March of Mankind.

We moved as the Spirit listed. *They* never altered their
pace,
Being neither cloud nor wind-borne like the Gods of the
Market-Place;
But they always caught up with our progress, and
presently word would come
That a tribe had been wiped off its icefield, or the lights
had gone out in Rome.

With the Hopes that our World is built on they were
utterly out of touch,
They denied that the Moon was Stilton; they denied she
was even Dutch.
They denied that Wishes were Horses; they denied that a
Pig had Wings.
So we worshipped the Gods of the Market Who promised
these beautiful things.

[153]

When the Cambrian measures were forming, They
  promised perpetual peace.
They swore, if we gave them our weapons, that the wars
  of the tribes would cease.
But when we disarmed They sold us and delivered us
  bound to our foe,
And the Gods of the Copybook Headings said: *'Stick to the
  Devil You know.'*

On the first Feminian Sandstones we were promised the
  Fuller Life
(Which started by loving our neighbour and ended by
  loving his wife)
Till our women had no more children and the men lost
  reason and faith,
And the Gods of the Copybook Headings said: *'The Wages
  of Sin is Death.'*

In the Carboniferous Epoch we were promised abundance
  for all,
By robbing selected Peter to pay for collective Paul;
But, though we had plenty of money, there was nothing
  our money could buy,
And the Gods of the Copybook Headings said: *'If you don't
  work you die.'*

Then the Gods of the Market tumbled, and their smooth-
  tongued wizards withdrew,
And the hearts of the meanest were humbled and began to
  believe it was true
That All is not Gold that Glitters, and Two and Two make
  Four—
And the Gods of the Copybook Headings limped up to
  explain it once more.
  .   .   .   .

*We are still busy
doing this, I notice! —
as enthusiastically
as ever.*

[154]

As it will be in the future, it was at the birth of Man—
There are only four things certain since Social Progress
       began:—
That the Dog returns to his Vomit and the Sow returns to
      her Mire,
And the burnt Fool's bandaged finger goes wabbling back
      to the Fire;

And that after this is accomplished, and the brave new
      world begins
When all men are paid for existing and no man must pay
      for his sins,
As surely as Water will wet us, as surely as Fire will burn,
The Gods of the Copybook Headings with terror and
      slaughter return!

The line about the burnt Fool's finger, never fails to remind me of Angelina; a common brown monkey who was found in the jungle, as a tiny baby still clinging to her dead mother, and presented by her finders to my sister and myself. We kept her for years.

One hard winter, spent in snowbound Kashmir, we had a circular wood-burning stove in our playroom, and the first day it was installed Angie put out a hand and touched it—and yelled the roof off! Well, you'd think that would have taught her, but not a bit of it. Believe it or not, every single day of that long winter she would prance into the room and circle the stove, considering this hostile object that had assaulted her. Would it do so again? Or not?

It seemed she had to find out; and always unable to resist, she burned her paw—for the umpteenth time!

[155]

'NON NOBIS DOMINE!'

Non nobis Domine!—
  Not unto us, O Lord!
The Praise or Glory be
  Of any deed or word;
For in Thy Judgment lies
  To crown or bring to nought
All knowledge or device
  That Man has reached or wrought.

And we confess our blame—
  How all too high we hold
That noise which men call Fame,
  That dross which men call Gold.
For these we undergo
  Our hot and godless days,
But in our hearts we know
  Not unto us the Praise.

O Power by Whom we live—
  Creator, Judge, and Friend,
Upholdingly forgive
  Nor fail us at the end:
But grant us well to see
  In all our piteous ways—
Non nobis Domine!—
  Not unto us the Praise!

SESTINA OF
THE TRAMP-ROYAL

Speakin' in general, I 'ave tried 'em all—
The 'appy roads that take you o'er the world.
Speakin' in general, I 'ave found them good
For such as cannot use one bed too long,
But must get 'ence, the same as I 'ave done,
An' go observin' matters till they die.

What do it matter where or 'ow we die,
So long as we've our 'ealth to watch it all—
The different ways that different things are done,
An' men an' women lovin' in this world;
Takin' our chances as they come along,
An' when they ain't, pretendin' they are good?

In cash or credit—no, it aren't no good;
You 'ave to 'ave the 'abit or you'd die,
Unless you lived your life but one day long,
Nor didn't prophesy nor fret at all,
But drew your tucker some'ow from the world,
An' never bothered what you might ha' done.

But, Gawd, what things are they I 'aven't done?
I've turned my 'and to most, an' turned it good,
In various situations round the world—
For 'im that doth not work must surely die;
But that's no reason man should labour all
'Is life on one same shift—life's none so long.

Therefore, from job to job I've moved along.
Pay couldn't 'old me when my time was done,
For something in my 'ead upset it all,
Till I 'ad dropped whatever 'twas for good,
An', out at sea, be'eld the dock-lights die,
An' met my mate—the wind that tramps the world!

[157]

During my school-
days, like so many
of us I had a stab
at writing poetry,
and how well
I remember
wrestling with those
wretched sonnets
and the discipline
they imposed.

I struggled on,
however, until the
Eng: Lit: teacher
advanced into
sestinas. At which
point I gave up.

The ease with which
Kipling's Tramp-
Royal speaks
within the strict
limits of a sestina
is fascinating—
one could almost
fail to notice that
he was doing so if
that word had
not been in the title.

As for that last line,
it would make
a wonderful epitaph
— I've liked it all
too!
Oh, how I've liked it!

It's like a book, I think, this bloomin' world,
Which you can read and care for just so long,
But presently you feel that you will die
Unless you get the page you're readin' done,
An' turn another—likely not so good;
But what you're after is to turn 'em all.

Gawd bless this world! Whatever she 'ath done—
Excep' when awful long—I've found it good.
So write, before I die, "E liked it all!'

[158]

INDEXES

INDEX OF TITLES

[160]

INDEX OF FIRST LINES